200 Adjectives 2,000 Sentences
Latin American Spanish
Frequency List

200 Adjectives 2,000 Sentences
Latin American Spanish
Frequency List

PRESS

ISBN: 978-1-952161-14-8

www.L2Press.com

First Edition

This Spanish book series is dedicated to

Alexander Argüelles, Luca Lampariello, and Mikel Telleria Mujika

for their practical contributions to self-taught language learners.

Thank you.

Introduction

This book introduces the 200 most frequent Spanish adjectives, which account for about 80% of the adjectives you'll encounter in everyday conversation and writing. Each adjective is presented through 10 simple example sentences that highlight its most common meaning and inflections. But you're not just learning adjectives in isolation. Each adjective appears alongside the words it frequently pairs with, including common nouns, verbs, adverbs, and prepositions that native speakers use all the time. As a result, you'll repeatedly see and absorb the vocabulary that most often appears with these high-frequency adjectives. Over the course of the book, this adds up to exposure to thousands of useful words and patterns. Think of this book not just as a guide to 200 adjectives, but as a gateway to the core vocabulary and patterns that shape natural, everyday Spanish.

The beauty of this method lies in its simplicity. Short, easy-to-understand sentences allow you to focus on building a solid foundation without feeling overwhelmed. Experienced language learners tend to make faster progress when they're exposed to large amounts of clear, understandable language rather than focusing heavily on grammar rules. With that in mind, you'll learn primarily through meaningful repetition and practical examples while developing the ability to infer meaning from context, one of the most valuable skills for long-term proficiency and fluency. By encountering words and structures repeatedly in various meaningful contexts, you'll gradually develop an intuitive feel for Spanish that goes beyond memorization.

By the time you complete this book and its companions, "200 Nouns" and "200 Verbs", you'll have built a vocabulary and intuition strong enough to dive into authentic content made for native Spanish speakers. While this book introduces many common nouns and adjectives in context, the companion books give them the dedicated, systematic treatment they deserve, ensuring the highest-frequency words in each category are fully covered, not just encountered in passing. Together, these three books cover the highest-frequency words across the most essential categories of Spanish, giving you a solid, well-rounded foundation.

The Spanish in this book reflects Latin American usage, with a slight emphasis on Mexico. The audio is read by a native Mexican speaker, so you'll hear a clear, neutral Mexican accent throughout. The vocabulary is easily understood across Latin America (and even Spain), while staying grounded in everyday Mexican usage. Mexico is home to more Spanish speakers than any other country, making its variety of Spanish an ideal foundation for anyone learning the language.

Audio is where everything comes together. Reading helps you recognize patterns, but listening and speaking is what turns those patterns into real, usable language. When you hear the sentences spoken clearly and naturally, you begin to internalize pronunciation, rhythm, and flow. Your Spanish will start to feel more automatic and authentic. The complete audio for this book allows you to reinforce every sentence through repeated exposure, helping you connect what you see on the page with how it actually sounds. You can listen while reading, repeat aloud while reading, or listen on its own to train your ear. This kind of consistent repetition is the fastest way to build real fluency. If you want to move beyond recognizing Spanish to truly understanding and using it, combining the book with the audio is essential. The full audio of this book is available for purchase at L2Press.com.

Ready to start your Spanish journey the smart and efficient way? This book offers you a clear path to success. Whether your goal is to connect with Spanish-speaking friends, enhance your career opportunities, or immerse yourself in the rich culture of Mexico, Colombia, and other Spanish-speaking countries, this book will get you there faster and more effectively than traditional grammar-based approaches. Don't waste time on inefficient learning methods. Begin your transformation into a confident Spanish speaker today with this focused and practical approach to language learning.

How to use this book

Build Spanish fluency by rotating through three powerful techniques: shadowing, reading aloud, active recall:

- Shadowing is a form of active listening. Listen to the audio and repeat it aloud nearly simultaneously, following the speaker like a shadow. You can do this while reading the Spanish, the English, or without looking at the text. Focus on sounding like the native speaker. Pay attention to vowel sounds, vowel length, new consonant sounds, stress, and intonation.
- Reading aloud bridges the gap between written and spoken Spanish. Simply read the sentences out loud at your own pace. This helps you build confidence, improve pronunciation, and get used to hearing your own voice in Spanish.
- Active recall here means translating from English into Spanish. Cover the Spanish and try to produce the Spanish you've been practicing. It's the most effective and challenging step, as it forces your brain to retrieve the language instead of just recognizing it.

Note that you speak aloud in each step. This is critical for training your mouth and tongue. Language is a physical skill as much as a mental one, and your ability to understand and recall Spanish will only take you so far if your mouth isn't trained to produce it. Whether you are shadowing, reading aloud, or doing active recall, speaking in every step builds the muscle memory needed to form sounds quickly, smoothly, and naturally. This repeated, active production is what turns passive knowledge into real speaking ability.

These three techniques work together as a single learning loop that you repeat with the same material. Rather than moving on to new material each day, you return to the same sentences in different ways. You begin by hearing and imitating the language through shadowing, which builds familiarity with the sounds and rhythm. Then you reinforce that familiarity by reading aloud at your own pace, giving your brain more time to process and your mouth more time to practice. Finally, you test and strengthen what you've learned through active recall, forcing yourself to produce the language on your own. Each step prepares you for the next, and each pass through the loop deepens your understanding and ability. Over time, what once felt unfamiliar will become more automatic.

I recommend spending about 30 minutes per day with this book. On the first day, shadow six pages. On the second day, go back to those same six pages and read them aloud at your own pace. On the third day, cover the Spanish and try to actively recall the sentences by translating from English. If you can produce at least half of them with reasonable accuracy, that's a good sign you're ready to move on to the next set of pages. If not, simply repeat the cycle. There's no need to rush. Going back over the same material is not a setback. It's how you learn. Some sections will click quickly, while others may take an extra pass or two. The goal is steady progress and growing familiarity, not perfection.

Your goal is not to memorize every sentence in this book. Your goal is exposure. By working through many examples of the most common verbs and structures, you start to recognize patterns without having to think about them. You'll encounter the same words and constructions multiple times in slightly different contexts, and your brain will absorb them naturally over time. Some sentences will stick and others won't, and that's perfectly fine. What matters is building a deep familiarity with how Spanish works. That familiarity is what allows you to understand real Spanish and respond with confidence.

Recommended routine

A 3-day loop that will produce excellent results (Day 1 - Shadow, Day 2 - Read aloud, Day 3 - Active recall):

Day 1 of pages **1-6**	Shadow **Spanish** twice (first while looking at Spanish & then while looking at English)
Day 2 of pages **1-6**	Read **Spanish** aloud, look at English translation, read Spanish aloud again
Day 3 of pages **1-6**	Active recall (cover the Spanish and translate the English into Spanish aloud)
Day 1 of pages 7-12	Shadow **Spanish** twice (first while looking at Spanish & then while looking at English)
Day 2 of pages 7-12	Read **Spanish** aloud, look at English translation, read Spanish aloud again
Day 3 of pages 7-12	Active recall (cover the Spanish and translate the English into Spanish aloud)
Day 1 of pages **13-18**	Shadow **Spanish** twice (first while looking at Spanish & then while looking at English)
Day 2 of pages **13-18**	Read **Spanish** aloud, look at English translation, read Spanish aloud again
Day 3 of pages **13-18**	Active recall (cover the Spanish and translate the English into Spanish aloud)
Day 1 of pages **19-24**	Shadow **Spanish** twice (first while looking at Spanish & then while looking at English)
Day 2 of pages **19-24**	Read **Spanish** aloud, look at English translation, read Spanish aloud again
Day 3 of pages **19-24**	Active recall (cover the Spanish and translate the English into Spanish aloud)
Day 1 of pages 25-30	Shadow **Spanish** twice (first while looking at Spanish & then while looking at English)
Day 2 of pages 25-30	Read **Spanish** aloud, look at English translation, read Spanish aloud again
Day 3 of pages 25-30	Active recall (cover the Spanish and translate the English into Spanish aloud)
Day 1 of pages 31-36	Shadow **Spanish** twice (first while looking at Spanish & then while looking at English)
Day 2 of pages 31-36	Read **Spanish** aloud, look at English translation, read Spanish aloud again
Day 3 of pages 31-36	Active recall (cover the Spanish and translate the English into Spanish aloud)
Day 1 of pages 37-42	Shadow **Spanish** twice (first while looking at Spanish & then while looking at English)
Day 2 of pages 37-42	Read **Spanish** aloud, look at English translation, read Spanish aloud again
Day 3 of pages 37-42	Active recall (cover the Spanish and translate the English into Spanish aloud)
Day 1 of pages **43-48**	Shadow **Spanish** twice (first while looking at Spanish & then while looking at English)
Day 2 of pages **43-48**	Read **Spanish** aloud, look at English translation, read Spanish aloud again
Day 3 of pages **43-48**	Active recall (cover the Spanish and translate the English into Spanish aloud)
Day 1 of pages **49-54**	Shadow **Spanish** twice (first while looking at Spanish & then while looking at English)
Day 2 of pages **49-54**	Read **Spanish** aloud, look at English translation, read Spanish aloud again
Day 3 of pages **49-54**	Active recall (cover the Spanish and translate the English into Spanish aloud)
Day 1 of pages 55-60	Shadow **Spanish** twice (first while looking at Spanish & then while looking at English)
Day 2 of pages 55-60	Read **Spanish** aloud, look at English translation, read Spanish aloud again
Day 3 of pages 55-60	Active recall (cover the Spanish and translate the English into Spanish aloud)
Day 1 of pages 61-67	Shadow **Spanish** twice (first while looking at Spanish & then while looking at English)
Day 2 of pages 61-67	Read **Spanish** aloud, look at English translation, read Spanish aloud again
Day 3 of pages 61-67	Active recall (cover the Spanish and translate the English into Spanish aloud)

What to do after this book series

This book series gives you a strong, intermediate-level foundation in Spanish. Once you finish it, the next step is to move into real-world Spanish, where your progress will come from continued exposure, active use, and consistent practice. Here are some of the most effective ways to keep improving with native materials.

Reading: There are two main methods language learners use to read, intensive reading and extensive reading. Intensive reading means working through a small amount of text carefully, looking up words and paying attention to grammar and sentence structure. Extensive reading means reading quickly and fluidly for enjoyment, without stopping to look things up, to build overall exposure to the language. Do both. Read books written for native speakers, starting with simpler ones, and consider reading Spanish versions of books you've already read and know well. Choose topics and genres you enjoy. Over time, extensive reading builds familiarity with vocabulary and structure, while intensive reading helps you understand the details more deeply. Don't forget to read aloud some of the time.

Watching and Listening: Watch TV shows, movies, and listen to podcasts in Spanish on topics you already enjoy. In the beginning, look for simpler native content. Then gradually move on to more advanced content, even if you don't catch everything. To get the most out of any episode, read a transcript beforehand to prime your brain and familiarize yourself with new words and phrases. Then watch or listen attentively and review the transcript afterward. Repeat this process as often as you like, while also exposing yourself to a wide variety of content. Over time, your ear will adapt, your vocabulary will grow, and what once felt confusing will start to feel natural.

Speaking: Find a native speaker and converse with them on a consistent basis. The ideal practice partner is patient and will not simply correct your errors but will prompt you to self-correct and express your ideas more clearly. If you want to speak fluently, there is no substitute for regular conversation. Try to schedule consistent sessions, even if they are short, and focus on communicating your thoughts rather than speaking perfectly. Mistakes are part of the process. Prepare a few topics or questions beforehand to keep the conversation flowing, and reuse phrases you've learned so they become automatic. You will eventually notice that what once required effort starts to come naturally, and your confidence will grow with each interaction.

Language Islands: A language island is a personal collection of sentences built around specific situations in your own life, practiced until they become automatic so the language is already there when you need it. The idea is to build small islands of fluency around moments you're likely to find yourself in, such as introducing yourself, ordering food, talking about your work or your family. To create one, write about 20 simple, natural sentences you would actually say in that situation, then practice them out loud until they feel effortless. Eventually you can expand their complexity by adding details, changing verb tenses, and swapping vocabulary. Over time, your islands grow and connect, and your speech becomes faster, more natural, and more confident.

Travel and Immersion: Visit a Spanish-speaking country and avoid using any language but Spanish. When you're immersed, every interaction becomes a lesson. The pressure of real communication accelerates your progress in a way that structured study simply cannot. You will make mistakes and occasionally feel lost, but that discomfort is exactly what helps the language to click. Even short trips can lead to noticeable progress if you fully commit to using Spanish.

1 – bueno | **good**

El café de esta cafetería es muy bueno. | The coffee at this coffee shop is very good.
Mi papá es un buen cocinero. | My dad is a good cook.
Ese restaurante es muy bueno, deberías probarlo. | That restaurant is really good, you should try it.
Es una buena idea para el proyecto. | It's a good idea for the project.
Tienes una buena posibilidad de conseguir el trabajo. | You have a good chance of getting the job.
La película estuvo buena, me hizo reír mucho. | The movie was good, it made me laugh a lot.
¿Conoces algunos restaurantes buenos por aquí? | Do you know any good restaurants around here?
Los precios en esa tienda son muy buenos. | The prices at that store are very good.
Buenas tardes, ¿cómo estás? | Good afternoon, how are you?
Las noticias de hoy fueron buenas para la economía. | Today's news was good for the economy.

2 – grande | **big, large**

Vivo en una casa grande en las afueras. | I live in a big house in the suburbs.
Tenemos un televisor grande en la sala. | We have a big TV in the living room.
Fue un gran día para todos. | It was a great day for everyone.
¿Tienes una talla más grande? | Do you have a bigger size?
Tengo una familia grande. | I have a big family.
Tengo una gran sorpresa para ti. | I have a big surprise for you.
Los niños sueñan con ser grandes. | Children dream of being grown up.
Mis hijos ya están grandes. | My kids are already grown up.
Las ciudades grandes tienen mucho tráfico. | Big cities have a lot of traffic.
Las ventanas grandes dejan entrar mucha luz. | The big windows let in a lot of light.

3 – pequeño | **small, little**

Ese perro pequeño ladra mucho. | That little dog barks a lot.
Vivimos en un pueblo pequeño. | We live in a small town.
Mi hermano pequeño tiene seis años. | My little brother is six years old.
La casa es pequeña pero cómoda. | The house is small but comfortable.
La mesa pequeña cabe aquí perfectamente. | The small table fits perfectly here.
Mi hija más pequeña empezó el jardín. | My youngest daughter started kindergarten.
Estos zapatos son demasiado pequeños para mí. | These shoes are too small for me.
Los niños pequeños ya están dormidos. | The little kids are already asleep.
Tengo las manos pequeñas para mi estatura. | I have small hands for my height.
Las ciudades pequeñas tienen su encanto. | Small cities have their charm.

4 – importante	**important**
El médico dice que el descanso es importante.	The doctor says rest is important.
Tengo que decirte algo importante.	I have something important to tell you.
Lo más importante es que estés feliz.	The most important thing is that you're happy.
La decisión fue difícil pero importante.	The decision was difficult but important.
Mi mamá es la persona más importante de mi vida.	My mom is the most important person in my life.
La salud es más importante que el dinero.	Health is more important than money.
Estos cambios son importantes para la empresa.	These changes are important for the company.
Los valores familiares son importantes para nosotros.	Family values are important to us.
Las primeras impresiones son muy importantes.	First impressions are very important.
Mis amigas más importantes estuvieron en la boda.	My most important friends were at the wedding.

5 – nuevo	**new**
¿Ese es tu celular nuevo?	Is that your new phone?
El vecino nuevo se presentó ayer.	The new neighbor introduced himself yesterday.
¿Ya empezaste tu nuevo trabajo?	Did you already start your new job?
Estoy feliz con mi computadora nueva.	I'm happy with my new computer.
La película nueva de ese director es muy buena.	That director's new movie is really good.
Vamos a probar la pizzería nueva.	Let's try the new pizzeria.
Tenemos muebles nuevos en la sala.	We have new furniture in the living room.
Estos zapatos nuevos me están matando los pies.	These new shoes are killing my feet.
Compramos sillas nuevas para el comedor.	We bought new chairs for the dining room.
Sus canciones nuevas son pegajosas.	Her new songs are catchy.

6 – malo	**bad, mean**
Soy malo para recordar nombres.	I'm bad at remembering names.
Ese hombre es malo.	That man is mean.
Ese chico tiene muy malos modales.	That boy has very bad manners.
Es una mala película.	It's a bad movie.
Esa película fue mala de principio a fin.	That movie was bad from start to finish.
Es una mala idea manejar con este clima.	It's a bad idea to drive in this weather.
Me dieron malos consejos.	They gave me bad advice.
Es difícil dejar los malos hábitos.	It's difficult to quit bad habits.
Esas amigas son malas influencias.	Those friends are bad influences.
Tuvieron malas experiencias en ese hotel.	They had bad experiences at that hotel.

7 – feliz | **happy**

Soy feliz cuando paso tiempo con mis hijos. | I'm happy when I spend time with my kids.
Me siento feliz de estar vivo. | I feel happy to be alive.
¡Feliz cumpleaños! | Happy birthday!
Vivieron una vida feliz. | They lived a happy life.
Estoy feliz de que todo saliera bien. | I'm happy that everything turned out well.
Me hace feliz saber que estás bien. | It makes me happy to know you're okay.
Los niños se ven felices y saludables. | The children look happy and healthy.
Somos felices juntos. | We're happy together.
Las amigas están felices por el reencuentro. | The friends are happy about the reunion.
Las niñas volvieron felices de la fiesta. | The girls came back happy from the party.

8 – difícil | **difficult, hard**

Ese trabajo es difícil si no tienes experiencia. | That job is difficult if you don't have experience.
Es difícil concentrarse con tanto ruido. | It's hard to concentrate with so much noise.
Fue un año difícil para todos. | It was a tough year for everyone.
Mi suegra es una mujer difícil. | My mother-in-law is a difficult woman.
Esta materia es difícil si no estudias mucho. | This subject is difficult if you don't study a lot.
Esa decisión va a ser difícil. | That decision is going to be tough.
Los idiomas pueden ser difíciles al principio. | Languages can be difficult at first.
Los tiempos son difíciles para todos. | Times are tough for everyone.
Las preguntas del examen estuvieron muy difíciles. | The exam questions were very hard.
Mis materias este semestre están muy difíciles. | My subjects this semester are very difficult.

9 – joven | **young**

Un hombre joven me ayudó a cargar las bolsas. | A young man helped me carry the bags.
El cantante joven se hizo famoso rápido. | The young singer became famous quickly.
Un doctor joven me examinó en el hospital. | A young doctor examined me at the hospital.
La actriz joven ganó un premio. | The young actress won an award.
Ella es demasiado joven para manejar. | She's too young to drive.
Sigo sintiéndome joven a pesar de los años. | I still feel young despite the years.
Mis papás se casaron jóvenes. | My parents got married young.
Se ven muy jóvenes para su edad. | They look very young for their age.
Conocí a unas artistas jóvenes en la feria. | I met some young artists at the fair.
Mis sobrinas jóvenes ya tienen celular. | My young nieces already have cell phones.

10 – inteligente | **intelligent, smart**

El perro es inteligente, aprende trucos fácilmente. | The dog is smart, it learns tricks easily.
Mi abuelo era inteligente y sabio. | My grandfather was intelligent and wise.
Es inteligente pedir ayuda cuando la necesitas. | It's smart to ask for help when you need it.
Tu hermana es inteligente y trabajadora. | Your sister is intelligent and hardworking.
Es una mujer inteligente y segura de sí misma. | She's a smart woman and confident in herself.
Fue una decisión inteligente ahorrar ese dinero. | Saving that money was a smart decision.
Los gemelos son igual de inteligentes. | The twins are equally smart.
Mis hijos son inteligentes pero perezosos. | My sons are smart but lazy.
Estas respuestas son muy inteligentes. | These answers are very smart.
Mis hermanas son inteligentes y ambiciosas. | My sisters are intelligent and ambitious.

11 – mejor | **better, best**

Ese es el mejor lugar para comer tacos. | That's the best place to eat tacos.
¿Quién es tu mejor amigo? | Who is your best friend?
Mi hijo es el mejor estudiante de su clase. | My son is the best student in his class.
La segunda película fue mejor que la primera. | The second movie was better than the first one.
Mi mamá hace la mejor comida del mundo. | My mom makes the best food in the world.
¿Cuál es la mejor opción para nosotros? | Which is the best option for us?
Mis mejores recuerdos son de la infancia. | My best memories are from childhood.
Estos son los mejores tacos de la ciudad. | These are the best tacos in the city.
Las frutas maduras son mejores para el jugo. | Ripe fruits are better for juice.
Las mejores cosas de la vida son gratis. | The best things in life are free.

12 – viejo | **old**

Mi gato viejo duerme todo el día. | My old cat sleeps all day.
El edificio viejo necesita reparaciones. | The old building needs repairs.
El árbol viejo del parque tiene más de cien años. | The old tree in the park is over a hundred years old.
Tengo ropa vieja que ya no uso. | I have old clothes that I no longer use.
La iglesia vieja del centro es muy bonita. | The old church downtown is very beautiful.
Esta lavadora vieja ya no funciona. | This old washing machine doesn't work anymore.
Guardamos juguetes viejos en el ático. | We keep old toys in the attic.
Los libros viejos tienen un olor distinto. | Old books have a distinct smell.
Estas fotos viejas me dan nostalgia. | These old photos make me nostalgic.
¿Por qué guardas esas revistas viejas? | Why do you keep those old magazines?

13 – último	**last, final**
¿Quién se comió el último pedazo de pastel?	Who ate the last piece of cake?
¿Cuándo es el último día de clases?	When is the last day of classes?
Este es el último capítulo de la serie.	This is the last episode of the series.
Esta es tu última oportunidad.	This is your last chance.
La última página del libro me hizo llorar.	The last page of the book made me cry.
Esa fue la última vez que lo vi.	That was the last time I saw him.
Mi hermano se comió los dos últimos tacos.	My brother ate the last two tacos.
Los últimos días han sido difíciles.	The last few days have been tough.
¿Cuáles fueron sus últimas palabras?	What were her final words?
¿Leíste las últimas noticias?	Did you read the latest news?

14 – posible	**possible**
No es posible entrar sin boleto.	It's not possible to enter without a ticket.
¿Es posible que llegues temprano mañana?	Is it possible for you to arrive early tomorrow?
No parece posible terminar hoy.	It doesn't seem possible to finish today.
La única explicación posible es que mintió.	The only possible explanation is that he lied.
Una explicación posible es que se le olvidó.	One possible explanation is that he forgot.
Una solución posible sería hablar con ella.	One possible solution would be to talk to her.
Hay varios caminos posibles para llegar allí.	There are several possible ways to get there.
Analizamos los efectos posibles del cambio.	We analyzed the possible effects of the change.
Revisamos todas las opciones posibles.	We went over all the possible options.
Hay dos soluciones posibles al conflicto.	There are two possible solutions to the conflict.

15 – alto	**tall, high, loud**
El edificio más alto de la ciudad tiene treinta pisos.	The tallest building in the city has thirty floors.
El precio de la gasolina está muy alto este mes.	The price of gasoline is very high this month.
El volumen está demasiado alto, bájale un poco.	The volume is way too loud, turn it down a bit.
Mi hija es alta, ya me llega hasta el hombro.	My daughter is tall, she already reaches my shoulder.
La probabilidad de lluvia hoy es alta, lleva paraguas.	The chance of rain today is high, take an umbrella.
Su voz es alta y se escucha desde lejos.	Her voice is loud and can be heard from far away.
Los rascacielos en esa ciudad son muy altos.	The skyscrapers in that city are very tall.
Los niveles de estrés en ese trabajo son muy altos.	The stress levels in that job are really high.
Las palmeras altas dan sombra en la playa.	The tall palm trees provide shade on the beach.
Las montañas altas siempre tienen nieve en la cima.	High mountains always have snow on the peak.

16 – bajo	**low, short**
Mi hermano es bajo pero muy fuerte.	My brother is short but very strong.
El techo es bajo, así que ten cuidado con la cabeza.	The ceiling is low, so watch your head.
El río está bajo por la sequía.	The river is low because of the drought.
Mi abuela es la más baja de la familia.	My grandmother is the shortest in the family.
La temperatura está baja para esta época del año.	The temperature is low for this time of year.
Tu presión está baja, por eso te sientes mareada.	Your blood pressure is low, that's why you feel dizzy.
Mis hijos son bajos como yo.	My children are short like me.
Los precios están bajos por el fin de temporada.	The prices are low because it's the end of the season.
Estas sillas son muy bajas para la mesa.	These chairs are too low for the table.
Las ventas están bajas desde enero.	Sales have been low since January.

17 – abierto	**open**
El banco está abierto hasta las cinco.	The bank is open until five o'clock.
Dejaste el refrigerador abierto otra vez.	You left the fridge open again.
Este lugar está abierto al público todos los días.	This place is open to the public every day.
La tienda está abierta hasta tarde.	The store is open until late.
Tuvimos una conversación muy abierta.	We had a very open conversation.
Mi hermana es muy abierta con sus sentimientos.	My sister is very open with her feelings.
Los museos estarán abiertos el fin de semana.	The museums will be open on the weekend.
Estamos muy abiertos a sugerencias.	We are very open to suggestions.
Las puertas estaban abiertas cuando llegamos.	The doors were open when we arrived.
Tengo las ventanas abiertas para que entre aire.	I have the windows open so air can come in.

18 – barato	**cheap**
Este mercado es barato para frutas y verduras.	This market is cheap for fruits and vegetables.
Este restaurante es barato y la comida es deliciosa.	This restaurant is cheap and the food is delicious.
El vuelo salió barato porque lo compré antes.	The flight was cheap because I bought it early.
La comida callejera es barata y sabrosa aquí.	Street food is cheap and tasty here.
La universidad pública es más barata que la privada.	Public university is cheaper than private university.
La gasolina está más barata este mes que el anterior.	Gas is cheaper this month than last month.
Esos zapatos están baratos, pero no se ven buenos.	Those shoes are cheap, but they don't look good.
Los restaurantes baratos a veces son los mejores.	Cheap restaurants are sometimes the best.
Compré estas chanclas baratas para ir a la playa.	I bought these cheap flip-flops to go to the beach.
Busco opciones baratas para las vacaciones.	I'm looking for cheap vacation options.

19 – aburrido | **boring, bored**

Estoy aburrido en casa sin nada que hacer.	I'm bored at home with nothing to do.
Este programa de televisión es muy aburrido.	This TV show is very boring.
Ese profesor es tan aburrido que me quedo dormido.	That professor is so boring that I fall asleep.
María se siente aburrida en las reuniones familiares.	María feels bored at family gatherings.
La conferencia fue aburrida desde el principio.	The conference was boring from the beginning.
Esta canción es aburrida, cambia de emisora.	This song is boring, change the station.
Mis padres se ven aburridos viendo las noticias.	My parents look bored watching the news.
Los días lluviosos son muy aburridos.	Rainy days are so boring.
Estas clases son aburridas, no aprendo nada nuevo.	These classes are boring, I don't learn anything new.
Las tareas repetitivas son aburridas.	Repetitive tasks are boring.

20 – rico | **rich, tasty, delicious**

¡Qué rico!	How delicious!
Mi tío es rico y vive en Barcelona.	My uncle is rich and lives in Barcelona.
El jugo de naranja fresco está rico.	The fresh orange juice is tasty.
La pizza no es tan rica cuando está fría.	Pizza isn't as tasty when it's cold.
Esa familia es rica.	That family is rich.
La comida de mi abuela siempre queda rica.	My grandma's food always turns out delicious.
Son ricos.	They're rich.
Estos tacos están muy ricos.	These tacos are really tasty.
Las galletas caseras están ricas.	The homemade cookies are tasty.
Las personas ricas no siempre son felices.	Rich people aren't always happy.

21 – feo | **ugly**

El vestido está bonito, pero el color es feo.	The dress is pretty, but the color is ugly.
El golpe estuvo feo, pero él está bien.	The hit was ugly, but he's fine.
El perro del vecino es feo pero amigable.	The neighbor's dog is ugly but friendly.
La casa de la esquina es fea.	The house on the corner is ugly.
La situación se puso fea.	The situation got ugly.
Mi hermana cree que se ve fea sin maquillaje.	My sister thinks she looks ugly without makeup.
Esos zapatos están feos, cómprate otros.	Those shoes are ugly, buy different ones.
Los colores de esa pared se ven feos juntos.	The colors on that wall look ugly together.
Las discusiones se pusieron feas.	The arguments got ugly.
Las calles están feas con tanta basura.	The streets are ugly with so much trash.

22 – pobre | **poor**

Mi papá era pobre cuando era joven. | My dad was poor when he was young.
El pobre niño se cayó y se raspó la rodilla. | The poor boy fell and scraped his knee.
Ese pobre perro estaba temblando de frío. | That poor dog was shivering from the cold.
Mi abuela era muy pobre en su juventud. | My grandmother was very poor in her youth.
Esa pobre niña perdió a su gatito. | That poor girl lost her kitten.
La pobre María trabaja día y noche sin descanso. | Poor María works day and night without rest.
Mis abuelos eran pobres pero felices. | My grandparents were poor but happy.
Pobres chicos, les cancelaron la excursión. | Poor kids, their outing got canceled.
Las pobres gemelas tienen gripe al mismo tiempo. | The poor twins have the flu at the same time.
Las familias pobres reciben ayuda del gobierno. | Poor families receive help from the government.

23 – único | **unique, only**

Soy hijo único. | I'm an only child.
Ese artista tiene un estilo único. | That artist has a unique style.
El mole tiene un sabor único. | Mole has a unique flavor.
Ella es la única persona que me apoya. | She is the only person who supports me.
Esta es la única oportunidad que tenemos de ganar. | This is the only chance we have to win.
Ella es mi única amiga de la infancia. | She is my only childhood friend.
Son mis únicos amigos aquí. | They are my only friends here.
Mis únicos días libres son sábado y domingo. | My only days off are Saturday and Sunday.
Son las únicas fotos que tengo de ese viaje. | They're the only photos I have from that trip.
Estas fueron las únicas opciones que me dieron. | These were the only options they gave me.

24 – diferente | **different**

Este lugar se ve diferente desde la última vez. | This place looks different since the last time.
Busco algo diferente. | I'm looking for something different.
Mi hermano es muy diferente a mí. | My brother is very different from me.
Esta vez será diferente, te lo prometo. | This time will be different, I promise you.
Su opinión fue diferente a la mía. | Her opinion was different from mine.
La situación ahora es completamente diferente. | The situation now is completely different.
Todos tenemos caminos diferentes en la vida. | We all have different paths in life.
Hay diferentes maneras de resolver esto. | There are different ways to solve this.
Mis hermanas tienen personalidades diferentes. | My sisters have different personalities.
Las reglas son diferentes en cada país. | The rules are different in each country.

25 – especial — **special**

Mi abuelo fue alguien especial en mi vida. — My grandfather was someone special in my life.
Hoy es un día especial para nuestra familia. — Today is a special day for our family.
Mi papá tiene un talento especial para cocinar. — My dad has a special talent for cooking.
Tu amistad es muy especial para mí. — Your friendship is very special to me.
Esta canción es especial porque me recuerda a ti. — This song is special because it reminds me of you.
Ella ocupa un lugar especial en mi corazón. — She holds a special place in my heart.
Estos momentos son especiales para recordar. — These moments are special to remember.
Tenemos descuentos especiales para clientes nuevos. — We have special discounts for new customers.
Tuve muchas experiencias especiales durante mi infancia. — I had many special experiences during my childhood.
Guardamos fotos especiales del viaje en un álbum. — We kept special photos from the trip in an album.

26 – mayor — **older, bigger, major**

El problema mayor es la falta de dinero. — The biggest problem is the lack of money.
Mi hermano mayor vive en otra ciudad. — My older brother lives in another city.
Soy tres años y medio mayor que mi esposa. — I am three and a half years older than my wife.
Mi hermana mayor me enseñó a manejar. — My older sister taught me to drive.
La preocupación mayor es la salud de mi mamá. — The biggest concern is my mom's health.
La hija mayor cuida a sus hermanos. — The oldest daughter takes care of her siblings.
Mis primos mayores son como hermanos para mí. — My older cousins are like siblings to me.
Mis hermanos mayores ya se fueron de casa. — My older siblings have already left home.
Las personas mayores tienen descuento en el autobús. — Senior citizens receive a discount on the bus.
Mis hermanas mayores ya son mamás. — My older sisters are already moms.

27 – largo — **long**

Mi cabello está muy largo, necesito cortarlo. — My hair is very long, I need to cut it.
Tu discurso estuvo un poco largo. — Your speech was a little long.
El río es largo y atraviesa todo el país. — The river is long and crosses the entire country.
La carrera estuvo larga pero terminé. — The race was long but I finished.
La reunión de trabajo fue larga y aburrida. — The work meeting was long and boring.
Esa mesa larga no cabe en mi comedor. — That long table doesn't fit in my dining room.
Los viajes largos me cansan. — Long trips tire me out.
Los pantalones me quedan largos. — The pants are too long for me.
Las colas en ese restaurante siempre son largas. — The lines at that restaurant are always long.
Las mangas de esta camisa son demasiado largas. — The sleeves of this shirt are too long.

28 – libre

Estoy libre el viernes.
El asiento está libre.
¿Estás libre este fin de semana para ayudarme?
Me siento tan libre desde que dejé a mi novio.
Ella es libre de tomar sus propias decisiones.
Ella es libre de irse cuando quiera.
Mis días libres son el sábado y el domingo.
Los asientos del fondo están libres.
Todas las personas deben ser libres.
Paso mis tardes libres con mi familia.

free, available

I'm free on Friday.
The seat is free.
Are you free this weekend to help me?
I feel so free since I left my boyfriend.
She is free to make her own decisions.
She is free to leave whenever she wants.
My days off are Saturday and Sunday.
The seats in the back are free.
All people should be free.
I spend my free afternoons with my family.

29 – seguro

Un banco es un lugar seguro para guardar tu dinero.
¿Es este un barrio seguro?
Este es el carro más seguro del mercado.
Usa una contraseña más segura.
Él tomó una decisión segura.
¿Estás segura de que quieres renunciar?
Estos son productos seguros para niños.
Hay pocos empleos seguros hoy en día.
Hay pocas zonas seguras en la ciudad.
Busco rutas seguras para correr.

safe, sure

A bank is a safe place to keep your money.
Is this a safe neighborhood?
This is the safest car on the market.
Use a more secure password.
He made a safe choice.
Are you sure you want to quit?
These are safe products for children.
There are few secure jobs nowadays.
There are few safe areas in the city.
I'm looking for safe routes for running.

30 – solo

El parque estaba solo a esa hora.
¿Viniste solo o con tu familia?
Estoy solo en casa esta noche.
Ella fue sola a la fiesta.
Caminamos por una calle sola.
Soy introvertida y prefiero estar sola.
No dejen a los perros solos tanto tiempo.
Los niños están solos en casa.
Ellas viven solas en ese departamento.
Las chicas no deberían andar solas de noche.

alone

The park was empty at that hour.
Did you come alone or with your family?
I'm home alone tonight.
She went to the party alone.
We walked down an empty street.
I'm an introvert and prefer to be alone.
Don't leave the dogs alone so long.
The children are alone at home.
They live on their own in that apartment.
Girls shouldn't wander around alone at night.

31 – fácil | **easy**

No es fácil decir que no. | It's not easy to say no.
Ganarle a ese equipo no será fácil. | Beating that team won't be easy.
No es fácil encontrar trabajo hoy en día. | It's not easy to find work nowadays.
Esta receta es fácil de hacer. | This recipe is easy to make.
Esa pregunta es fácil de responder. | That question is easy to answer.
La solución parece fácil. | The solution seems easy.
Los pasos son fáciles de seguir. | The steps are easy to follow.
Estos ejercicios están muy fáciles. | These exercises are really easy.
Las instrucciones son fáciles de entender. | The instructions are easy to understand.
Las materias fáciles me aburren. | Easy subjects bore me.

32 – común | **common**

Es un error común confundir esos términos. | It's a common mistake to confuse those terms.
Es común ver lluvia en esta época del año. | It's common to see rain at this time of year.
El miedo al cambio es un sentimiento común. | Fear of change is a common feeling.
Eso no es tan común como crees. | That's not as common as you think.
La causa más común de ese problema es el estrés. | The most common cause of that problem is stress.
La gripe es una enfermedad común. | The flu is a common illness.
Esos problemas son comunes en casas antiguas. | Those problems are common in old houses.
Son apellidos muy comunes en México. | They are very common surnames in Mexico.
Son palabras comunes en el español cotidiano. | They are common words in everyday Spanish.
Estas plantas son comunes en toda la región. | These plants are common throughout the region.

33 – interesante | **interesting**

El profesor nos contó algo interesante en clase. | The teacher told us something interesting in class.
Ese lugar tiene un pasado interesante. | That place has an interesting past.
Este libro es muy interesante, no lo puedo soltar. | This book is very interesting, I can't put it down.
Esa idea suena interesante, cuéntame más. | That idea sounds interesting, tell me more.
La exposición del museo estuvo bastante interesante. | The museum exhibition was quite interesting.
Esta receta se ve interesante, voy a probarla. | This recipe looks interesting, I'm going to try it.
Los comentarios del público fueron interesantes. | The audience's comments were interesting.
Los resultados del estudio son bastante interesantes. | The study results are quite interesting.
¿Tienes algunas fotos interesantes del viaje? | Do you have any interesting photos from the trip?
Esas películas no me parecen interesantes. | Those movies don't seem interesting to me.

34 – fuerte	**strong**
El café está muy fuerte hoy.	The coffee is very strong today.
Mi primo levanta pesas y es fuerte.	My cousin lifts weights and is strong.
El ruido fuerte del camión me despertó.	The loud noise from the truck woke me up.
La tormenta estuvo fuerte anoche.	The storm was strong last night.
Mi hija de cinco años tiene una personalidad fuerte.	My five-year-old daughter has a strong personality.
Mi abuela fue una mujer sorprendentemente fuerte.	My grandmother was a surprisingly strong woman.
Los olores fuertes me dan náuseas.	Strong smells make me nauseous.
Los ruidos fuertes asustaron al perro.	The loud noises scared the dog.
Las olas están muy fuertes para nadar.	The waves are too strong for swimming.
Las lluvias fuertes inundaron la calle.	The heavy rains flooded the street.

35 – rápido	**fast, quick**
¿Conoces un método rápido para aprender español?	Do you know a quick method to learn Spanish?
El internet no es tan rápido aquí.	The internet isn't that fast here.
Mi hermano es el corredor más rápido del equipo.	My brother is the fastest runner on the team.
Esa ciclista es muy rápida en las subidas.	That cyclist is very fast on the climbs.
La solución rápida no resolvió el problema.	The quick solution didn't solve the problem.
La comida rápida no es saludable.	Fast food isn't healthy.
Los cambios rápidos en el clima son sorprendentes.	The quick changes in weather are surprising.
Los carros rápidos consumen más gasolina.	Fast cars use more gas.
Necesito unas vacaciones, aunque sean rápidas.	I need a vacation, even if it's a quick one.
Esas recetas son rápidas y fáciles de preparar.	Those recipes are quick and easy to prepare.

36 – frío	**cold**
El agua de la piscina está muy fría.	The pool water is really cold.
Hace mucho frío hoy, necesito un suéter.	It's very cold today, I need a sweater.
El agua del río está muy fría para nadar.	The river water is too cold for swimming.
No me gusta la pizza fría.	I don't like cold pizza.
La cerveza está fría, justo como me gusta.	The beer is cold, just how I like it.
¿Por qué esta habitación está tan fría?	Why is this room so cold?
Los inviernos fríos son comunes en esa región.	Cold winters are common in that region.
Los vientos fríos vienen del norte.	The cold winds come from the north.
Las noches son muy frías en diciembre.	The nights are very cold in December.
Compramos unas cervezas frías en la tienda.	We bought some cold beers at the store.

37 – bonito

Él me dijo algo muy bonito y me hizo sonreír.
Ese vestido te queda bonito.
Qué bonito día hace hoy.
Tienes una letra muy bonita.
Tu hermana es muy bonita.
La canción es bonita.
Tienen unos jardines bonitos en ese parque.
Me encantan esos zapatos, están muy bonitos.
¡Qué bonitas están las decoraciones navideñas!
Las fotos de tu viaje están muy bonitas.

pretty, beautiful, nice, lovely

He said something very nice to me and made me smile.
That dress looks pretty on you.
What a beautiful day it is today.
You have very nice handwriting.
Your sister is very pretty.
The song is beautiful.
They have some pretty gardens in that park.
I love those shoes, they're really nice.
How pretty the Christmas decorations are!
The photos from your trip are really nice.

38 – serio

¿Hablas en serio?
Mi hijo se ve serio en la foto.
Este es un problema serio.
La situación es más seria de lo que parece.
Tuve una conversación seria con mi mamá ayer.
Dame una respuesta seria, no excusas.
Los daños fueron serios después del terremoto.
Tenemos problemas serios en el trabajo.
Mis amigas son serias cuando se trata de estudiar.
Hay consecuencias serias por tus acciones.

serious

Are you serious?
My son looks serious in the picture.
This is a serious problem.
The situation is more serious than it seems.
I had a serious conversation with my mom yesterday.
Give me a serious answer, not excuses.
The damages were serious after the earthquake.
We have serious problems at work.
My friends are serious when it comes to studying.
There are serious consequences to your actions.

39 – triste

La película tuvo un final triste.
Qué triste que no podamos vernos más seguido.
Es un día triste para la familia.
Ella está muy triste por la ruptura.
La triste historia me hizo llorar.
Leí una novela triste pero hermosa.
Los recuerdos tristes a veces vuelven de repente.
Mis padres estaban tristes cuando me mudé.
Son historias tristes de la guerra.
Mis hermanas están tristes porque se murió su gato.

sad

The movie had a sad ending.
How sad that we can't see each other more often.
It's a sad day for the family.
She is very sad about the breakup.
The sad story made me cry.
I read a sad but beautiful novel.
Sad memories sometimes come back suddenly.
My parents were sad when I moved away.
They're sad stories from the war.
My sisters are sad because their cat died.

40 – claro	**clear, light**
El cielo está claro después de la tormenta.	The sky is clear after the storm.
El mensaje fue claro desde el principio.	The message was clear from the beginning.
Está claro que necesitamos más tiempo.	It's clear that we need more time.
Tengo una idea clara de lo que quiero.	I have a clear idea of what I want.
Su respuesta fue clara y directa.	Her answer was clear and direct.
Necesito una respuesta clara de tu parte.	I need a clear answer from you.
Los ejemplos que diste fueron muy claros.	The examples you gave were very clear.
Los ojos claros son poco comunes en mi familia.	Light eyes are uncommon in my family.
Las instrucciones no son muy claras.	The instructions aren't very clear.
Tienes ideas claras sobre el proyecto.	You have clear ideas about the project.

41 – completo	**complete, full, whole**
El informe está completo y listo para entregarse.	The report is complete and ready to turn in.
Voy a hacer un cambio completo a mi vida.	I'm going to make a complete change in my life.
El curso completo tarda un año en terminarse.	The full course takes a year to finish.
Mi hermana vio la serie completa en dos días.	My sister watched the entire series in two days.
Necesito una explicación completa de lo que pasó.	I need a complete explanation of what happened.
Mi colección ya está completa.	My collection is now complete.
Los documentos están completos y firmados.	The documents are complete and signed.
Los datos no están completos todavía.	The data isn't complete yet.
Sus respuestas fueron claras y completas.	Her answers were clear and complete.
Las temporadas completas están en Netflix.	The complete seasons are on Netflix.

42 – necesario	**necessary**
Un cambio es necesario para mejorar la situación.	A change is necessary to improve the situation.
El apoyo de todos es necesario en este proyecto.	Everyone's support is necessary in this project.
No es necesario que vengas si estás ocupado.	It's not necessary for you to come if you're busy.
La paciencia es necesaria con los niños pequeños.	Patience is necessary with small children.
La experiencia previa no es necesaria.	Previous experience is not necessary.
Es necesaria la inscripción para participar.	Registration is necessary to participate.
Los permisos necesarios tardan una semana.	The necessary permits take a week.
Estos cambios son necesarios para la empresa.	These changes are necessary for the company.
Estas medidas son necesarias por seguridad.	These measures are necessary for security.
Las vacunas son necesarias antes del viaje a África.	Vaccines are necessary before the trip to Africa.

43 – negro | **black**

Quiero un bolígrafo negro, no azul. | I want a black pen, not a blue one.
El café negro me despierta rápido. | Black coffee wakes me up fast.
El cabello negro de mi hermana es muy bonito. | My sister's black hair is very pretty.
Llevo puesto unos jeans y una camiseta negra. | I'm wearing some jeans and a black t-shirt.
Mi gata negra tuvo gatitos. | My black cat had kittens.
Mi mascota es una perra negra muy juguetona. | My pet is a very playful black dog.
En mi país, los gatos negros dan mala suerte. | In my country, black cats bring bad luck.
Los pantalones negros nunca pasan de moda. | Black pants never go out of style.
Las cortinas negras oscurecen el dormitorio. | The black curtains darken the bedroom.
Las faldas negras son prácticas. | Black skirts are practical.

44 – blanco | **white**

El vino blanco está frío en la nevera. | The white wine is cold in the refrigerator.
El mantel blanco le da un toque elegante a la mesa. | The white tablecloth gives the table an elegant touch.
El arroz blanco va bien con el pollo. | White rice goes well with the chicken.
La camisa blanca combina con casi todo. | The white shirt goes with almost anything.
Me encanta la arena blanca de esa playa. | I love the white sand on that beach.
La bandera blanca significa rendición. | The white flag means surrender.
Los zapatos blancos se ensucian rápido. | White shoes get dirty quickly.
Los glóbulos blancos defienden el cuerpo. | White blood cells defend the body.
Las flores blancas del jardín huelen rico. | The white flowers in the garden smell nice.
Las nubes blancas parecían algodón. | The white clouds looked like cotton.

45 – próximo | **next, near, close**

El próximo lunes tengo cita con el doctor. | Next Monday I have a doctor's appointment.
El cine queda en el próximo edificio. | The movie theater is in the next building.
El pueblo más próximo está a diez kilómetros. | The nearest town is ten kilometers away.
Para la próxima vez, cómprate algo diferente. | For next time, buy yourself something different.
Tenemos un examen la próxima semana. | We have an exam next week.
Nos vemos el próximo año, te voy a extrañar. | See you next year, I'm going to miss you.
Los próximos días serán muy fríos. | The next few days will be very cold.
Los próximos años serán importantes para mi carrera. | The next few years will be important for my career.
Voy a pasar mis próximas vacaciones en la playa. | I'm going to spend my next vacation at the beach.
Las próximas semanas voy a estar muy ocupada. | The next few weeks I'm going to be very busy.

46 – listo | **ready, smart, clever**

¿Estás listo? | Are you ready?
Estoy listo para salir. | I'm ready to leave.
El café estará listo en cinco minutos. | The coffee will be ready in five minutes.
La comida ya está lista. | The food is ready now.
Mi hija es muy lista para resolver problemas. | My daughter is very clever at solving problems.
María es muy lista en matemáticas. | María is very smart at math.
Los documentos están listos para ser firmados. | The documents are ready to be signed.
¿Están listos para el viaje? | Are you ready for the trip?
Las chicas están listas para bailar. | The girls are ready to dance.
Las maletas están listas para el vuelo. | The suitcases are ready for the flight.

47 – cierto | **certain, true, specific**

Lo que dijo Juan no es cierto. | What Juan said isn't true.
¿Es cierto que te vas a mudar a otra ciudad? | Is it true that you're moving to another city?
En cierto momento, todos nos sentimos perdidos. | At a certain moment, we all felt lost.
Hay cierta tensión entre ellos. | There's a certain tension between them.
La historia de mi abuela es cierta. | My grandmother's story is true.
No confío mucho en cierta persona del equipo. | I don't really trust a certain person on the team.
Ciertos alimentos me caen mal en el estómago. | Certain foods upset my stomach.
Hay ciertos temas que no discuto. | There are certain topics I don't discuss.
Evito ciertas calles de noche por seguridad. | I avoid certain streets at night for safety reasons.
En ciertas ocasiones es mejor callarse. | On certain occasions it's better to stay quiet.

48 – cansado | **tired**

Me siento cansado después del entrenamiento. | I feel tired after the workout.
El perro está cansado de correr por el parque. | The dog is tired from running in the park.
Estoy cansado de escuchar siempre la misma excusa. | I'm tired of always hearing the same excuse.
Te ves cansada. ¿Estás bien? | You look tired. Are you okay?
Estoy cansada, solo quiero acostarme un rato. | I'm tired, I just want to lie down for a bit.
La profesora se veía cansada al final del día. | The teacher looked tired at the end of the day.
Mis papás regresaron cansados del viaje. | My parents came back tired from the trip.
Los niños estaban cansados pero felices. | The kids were tired but happy.
Estaban cansadas de esperar tanto tiempo. | They were tired of waiting so long.
Mis amigas estaban cansadas después del concierto. | My friends were tired after the concert.

49 – caro | **expensive**

El pan está muy caro en ese supermercado. | Bread is very expensive at that supermarket.
El restaurante al que fuimos era bastante caro. | The restaurant we went to was pretty expensive.
Ese celular está carísimo para lo que ofrece. | That phone is really expensive for what it offers.
Esta crema es muy cara, pero funciona bien. | This cream is very expensive, but it works well.
La gasolina está más cara que nunca. | Gas is more expensive than ever.
La renta está cara en el centro de la ciudad. | Rent is expensive in the city center.
Los boletos al concierto estaban caros. | The concert tickets were expensive.
Los carros están caros por la inflación. | Cars are expensive because of inflation.
Las clases particulares son caras. | Private lessons are expensive.
Las casas en esa zona son muy caras. | The houses in that area are very expensive.

50 – delgado | **thin**

Ese muchacho es muy delgado pero fuerte. | That guy is really thin but strong.
Juan siempre ha sido delgado. | Juan has always been thin.
El cable delgado no aguanta tanto peso. | The thin cable can't support that much weight.
La actriz es muy delgada, parece una modelo. | The actress is very slim, she looks like a model.
Su cara delgada le da un aspecto elegante. | Her slim face gives her an elegant look.
Esa capa delgada de pintura no es suficiente. | That thin layer of paint isn't enough.
Los fideos delgados se cocinan más rápido. | The thin noodles cook faster.
Los árboles delgados se doblan con el viento. | The thin trees bend with the wind.
Las piernas de la modelo eran largas y delgadas. | The model's legs were long and thin.
Las paredes delgadas no aíslan bien el ruido. | The thin walls don't insulate noise well.

51 – gordo | **fat, thick**

Mi abuelo se puso gordo después de jubilarse. | My grandfather got fat after retiring.
Mi gato está gordo porque come mucho. | My cat is fat because he eats a lot.
Necesito un marcador gordo para el letrero. | I need a thick marker for the poster.
Mi tía está más gorda desde que dejó de fumar. | My aunt is fatter since she quit smoking.
La gallina gorda puso dos huevos. | The fat hen laid two eggs.
La panza gorda del perro se arrastra por el suelo. | The dog's fat belly drags on the ground.
Los cerdos gordos valen más en el mercado. | Fat pigs are worth more at market.
Sus brazos gordos no entran en la camisa. | His fat arms don't fit in the shirt.
Mis piernas gordas no entran en estos pantalones. | My fat legs don't fit in these pants.
Esas vacas gordas dan más leche. | Those fat cows give more milk.

52 – propio | **own, typical**

No es propio de él mentir así. | It's not like him to lie like that.
El cantante tiene un estilo propio. | The singer has a style of his own.
Es muy propio de ti. | It's so typical of you.
Lo hice por mi propia cuenta. | I did it on my own.
Prefiero usar mi propia computadora para trabajar. | I prefer to use my own computer for work.
Esa actitud no es propia de ti. | That attitude isn't like you.
Debes tomar tus propios apuntes en clase. | You should take your own notes in class.
Cada quien tiene sus propios problemas. | Everyone has their own problems.
Cada quien es responsable de sus propias acciones. | Everyone is responsible for their own actions.
Lo hizo con sus propias manos. | He made it with his own hands.

53 – público | **public**

El baño público está muy sucio. | The public bathroom is very dirty.
El transporte público es más barato que un taxi. | Public transportation is cheaper than a taxi.
La información ya es de conocimiento público. | The information is already public knowledge.
La biblioteca pública abre a las ocho. | The public library opens at eight.
La playa pública está cerrada hoy. | The public beach is closed today.
La universidad pública es gratuita aquí. | The public university is free here.
Los espacios públicos deben cuidarse. | Public spaces must be taken care of.
Los servicios públicos incluyen agua, luz y gas. | Public services include water, electricity, and gas.
Las escuelas públicas necesitan más fondos. | Public schools need more funding.
Las playas públicas son gratuitas. | Public beaches are free.

54 – nacional | **national**

El himno nacional se canta en cada partido. | The national anthem is sung at every game.
Mañana es día feriado nacional. | Tomorrow is a national holiday.
El parque nacional está cerrado por mantenimiento. | The national park is closed for maintenance.
La bandera nacional ondea en la plaza. | The national flag waves in the square.
La selección nacional femenina ganó el torneo. | The women's national team won the tournament.
La universidad nacional es muy prestigiosa. | The national university is very prestigious.
Visitamos tres parques nacionales en el viaje. | We visited three national parks on the trip.
Los parques nacionales son muy bonitos. | The national parks are very beautiful.
Las elecciones nacionales son cada cuatro años. | National elections are every four years.
Las encuestas nacionales muestran un empate. | National polls show a tie.

55 – disponible | **available**

Si estoy disponible el viernes, te aviso. | If I'm available on Friday, I'll let you know.
El médico no está disponible hasta el lunes. | The doctor isn't available until Monday.
El gerente no está disponible en este momento. | The manager is not available right now.
Mi madre está disponible para cuidar a los niños. | My mother is available to babysit the kids.
La silla junto a la ventana está disponible. | The seat by the window is available.
La doctora está disponible solo por las mañanas. | The doctor is only available in the mornings.
Mis amigos están disponibles después de las seis. | My friends are available after six.
Hay varios turnos disponibles esta semana. | There are several time slots available this week.
Hay más opciones disponibles en línea. | There are more options available online.
Estas fechas están disponibles para la boda. | These dates are available for the wedding.

56 – capaz | **capable, able**

¿Tú crees que él es capaz de mentir así? | Do you think he's capable of lying like that?
Ella es capaz de aprender rápido si se concentra. | She is able to learn quickly if she focuses.
Él es capaz de resolver cualquier problema solo. | He's capable of solving any problem on his own.
Mi mamá es capaz de hacer cinco cosas a la vez. | My mom is capable of doing five things at once.
Es una niña muy capaz para su edad. | She's a very capable girl for her age.
Ella es muy capaz, pero necesita más confianza. | She's very capable but needs more confidence.
Mis amigos son capaces de cualquier locura. | My friends are capable of any kind of craziness.
Solo los más capaces llegan a ese nivel. | Only the most capable make it to that level.
Las chicas del equipo son capaces y fuertes. | The girls on the team are capable and strong.
Las enfermeras de este hospital son muy capaces. | The nurses at this hospital are very capable.

57 – pasado | **past, last, expired**

El año pasado viajamos a México con la familia. | Last year we traveled to Mexico with the family.
El fin de semana pasado fuimos al cine. | Last weekend we went to the movies.
El verano pasado fue muy caluroso. | Last summer was very hot.
La semana pasada llovió mucho. | Last week it rained a lot.
Esta leche está pasada, huele muy mal. | This milk is expired, it smells really bad.
En la clase pasada aprendimos un nuevo tema. | In the last class we learned a new topic.
Mis errores pasados me enseñaron mucho. | My past mistakes taught me a lot.
Los meses pasados han sido difíciles. | The past months have been difficult.
Las experiencias pasadas me ayudaron. | Past experiences helped me.
Las generaciones pasadas eran más respetuosas. | Past generations were more respectful.

58 – cercano	**close, nearby**
Vivo en un pueblo cercano a la capital.	I live in a town close to the capital.
Él es muy cercano a su abuelo.	He is very close to his grandfather.
Tenemos un amigo cercano que nos puede ayudar.	We have a close friend who can help us.
Tenemos una relación muy cercana.	We have a very close relationship.
La escuela más cercana tiene una buena reputación.	The nearest school has a good reputation.
Mi hermana y yo tenemos una amistad cercana.	My sister and I have a close friendship.
Sus familiares más cercanos vinieron a la boda.	His closest relatives came to the wedding.
Mis amigos más cercanos vienen a la fiesta.	My closest friends are coming to the party.
Mis amigas cercanas saben todos mis secretos.	My close friends know all my secrets.
Las escuelas cercanas tienen lista de espera.	The nearby schools have waiting lists.

59 – actual	**current**
¿Cuál es tu dirección actual?	What's your current address?
El presidente actual tomó posesión el año pasado.	The current president took office last year.
Mi trabajo actual me gusta mucho.	I really like my current job.
La tecnología actual permite hacer cosas increíbles.	Current technology allows us to do incredible things.
A todos les cae bien mi novia actual.	Everybody likes my current girlfriend.
La situación actual del país es complicada.	The current situation in the country is complicated.
Los precios actuales están por las nubes.	Current prices are through the roof.
Los gobiernos actuales enfrentan muchos retos.	Current governments face many challenges.
Mis circunstancias actuales no me permiten viajar.	My current circumstances don't allow me to travel.
Las tendencias actuales me parecen raras.	Current trends seem strange to me.

60 – frecuente	**frequent**
Es frecuente que el metro se retrase en las mañanas.	The subway is frequently delayed in the mornings.
El contacto frecuente ayuda a mantener la amistad.	Frequent contact helps maintain the friendship.
Ese error es frecuente en los principiantes.	That mistake is frequent among beginners.
Sus dolores de cabeza son frecuentes.	His headaches are frequent.
El tráfico pesado es frecuente a las cinco.	Heavy traffic is frequent at five.
Es frecuente la pérdida de memoria en ancianos.	Memory loss is frequent in elderly people.
Los cortes de luz son frecuentes en esta zona.	Power outages are frequent in this area.
Sus cambios de opinión son frecuentes.	His opinion changes are frequent.
Las grandes tormentas son frecuentes en abril.	Big storms are frequent in April.
Las discusiones frecuentes debilitan la relación.	Frequent arguments weaken the relationship.

61 – igual | **equal, same**

Tu celular es igual al mío. | Your phone is the same as mine.
Ese carro es igual al que tenía mi papá. | That car is the same as the one my dad had.
Me da igual lo que digan. | I don't care what they say.
La temperatura está igual de fría que ayer. | The temperature is just as cold as yesterday.
Esa camisa es igual a la que yo compré. | That shirt is the same as the one I bought.
La regla es igual para todos, no hay excepciones. | The rule is the same for everyone, no exceptions.
Los precios están iguales en ambas tiendas. | The prices are the same in both stores.
Todos somos iguales ante la ley. | We are all equal before the law.
Mis notas fueron iguales este semestre. | My grades were the same this semester.
Las dos fotos son iguales, no veo diferencia. | The two photos are the same, I see no difference.

62 – honesto | **honest**

Mi papá fue un hombre honesto. | My dad was an honest man.
El chico fue honesto sobre lo que pasó. | The boy was honest about what happened.
Para ser honesto, no quiero ir. | To be honest, I don't want to go.
Su respuesta fue honesta pero dolorosa. | Her answer was honest but painful.
Es una mujer honesta y trabajadora. | She's an honest, hardworking woman.
Necesitamos una conversación honesta sobre esto. | We need to have an honest conversation about this.
Mis padres siempre fueron honestos conmigo. | My parents were always honest with me.
Los políticos honestos son difíciles de encontrar. | Honest politicians are hard to find.
Las empresas honestas pagan sus impuestos completos. | Honest companies pay their taxes in full.
Las personas honestas siempre dicen la verdad. | Honest people always tell the truth.

63 – divertido | **fun, enjoyable, entertaining**

Ese videojuego es muy divertido. | That video game is really fun.
Tu primo es divertido, me cae bien. | Your cousin is fun, I like him.
El concierto estuvo muy divertido. | The concert was really fun.
La fiesta estuvo muy divertida. | The party was really fun.
La obra de teatro estuvo divertida. | The play was entertaining.
La conversación estuvo divertida. | The conversation was enjoyable.
Los deportes son divertidos si juegas en equipo. | Sports are fun if you play on a team.
Los juegos de mesa son divertidos. | Board games are fun.
Las actividades del campamento estuvieron divertidas. | The camp activities were fun.
Las salidas con amigos siempre son divertidas. | Going out with friends is always fun.

64 – limpio | **clean**

Me gusta mantener mi escritorio limpio. | I like to keep my desk clean.
Limpié el baño y ahora está limpio. | I cleaned the bathroom and now it's clean.
El juego fue limpio, sin faltas ni trampas. | The game was fair, without fouls or cheating.
Una casa limpia siempre me tranquiliza. | A clean house always calms me down.
La herida debe mantenerse limpia. | The wound must be kept clean.
La cocina está limpia después de ordenarla. | The kitchen is clean after tidying up.
Los carros limpios se venden más rápido. | Clean cars sell faster.
Necesitamos mantener limpios los espacios públicos. | We need to keep public spaces clean.
Las paredes se ven limpias con la nueva pintura. | The walls look clean with the new paint.
Las sábanas están limpias, acabo de cambiarlas. | The sheets are clean, I just changed them.

65 – enfermo | **sick, ill**

Mi papá está enfermo y no puede ir a trabajar. | My dad is sick and can't go to work.
Me sentí enfermo después de comer mariscos. | I felt sick after eating seafood.
Mi hijo está enfermo y no fue a la escuela. | My son is sick and didn't go to school.
Mi mamá se ha estado sintiendo enferma desde la mañana. | My mom has been feeling sick since morning.
La abuela está muy enferma en el hospital. | Grandma is very sick in the hospital.
La profesora vino incluso estando enferma. | The teacher came even though she was sick.
Algunos jugadores están enfermos y no jugarán. | Some players are sick and won't play.
Todos en la oficina están enfermos esta semana. | Everyone at the office is sick this week.
Las niñas están enfermas y no pueden salir. | The girls are sick and can't go out.
Las niñas enfermas tienen fiebre y tos. | The sick girls have a fever and cough.

66 – amable | **kind, nice**

Tu hermano es amable, me cae muy bien. | Your brother is nice, I like him a lot.
El doctor fue amable y me explicó todo. | The doctor was kind and explained everything to me.
Es un hombre amable que nunca niega favores. | He's a kind man who never refuses favors.
La profesora es amable, pero estricta con las tareas. | The teacher is kind but strict about homework.
Fue muy amable de su parte invitarnos a cenar. | It was very kind of her to invite us to dinner.
La recepcionista fue amable, pero no ayudó. | The receptionist was nice but didn't help.
Mis vecinos parecen muy amables. | My neighbors seem very kind.
Fueron muy amables por esperarnos una hora más. | They were very kind to wait an extra hour for us.
Las señoras de la panadería siempre son amables. | The ladies at the bakery are always nice.
Los empleados del hotel fueron amables y atentos. | The hotel staff were kind and attentive.

67 – hermoso | **beautiful, gorgeous, lovely**

El paisaje de la montaña es hermoso. | The mountain landscape is beautiful.
Me encanta tu jardín, está hermoso. | I love your garden, it's beautiful.
Qué vestido tan hermoso compraste. | What a beautiful dress you bought.
Tu hija se ve hermosa con ese vestido. | Your daughter looks gorgeous in that dress.
La vista desde aquí es hermosa. | The view from here is beautiful.
Soy afortunado de tener una familia hermosa. | I am fortunate to have a beautiful family.
Tenemos hermosos recuerdos de ese viaje. | We have beautiful memories from that trip.
Tus nietos son hermosos. | Your grandchildren are beautiful.
Mi ciudad tiene hermosas tradiciones. | My town has beautiful traditions.
Las flores del jardín están hermosas. | The flowers in the garden are beautiful.

68 – útil | **useful**

Una balanza es útil para medir ingredientes. | A scale is useful for measuring ingredients.
Ese curso tiene contenido útil. | That course has useful content.
Dame un regalo útil, no otra taza. | Give me a useful gift, not another mug.
Me dio información útil. | He gave me useful information.
Una aplicación útil es la que te ahorra tiempo. | A useful app is one that saves you time.
Esta es la guía más útil para recorrer Costa Rica. | This is the most useful guide for exploring Costa Rica.
Mi abuela siempre tiene consejos útiles. | My grandma always has useful advice.
Los ejemplos útiles ayudan a entender mejor. | Useful examples help to understand better.
Mi abuelo tiene un montón de herramientas útiles. | My grandpa has a ton of useful tools.
No aprendo habilidades útiles en la escuela. | I don't learn useful skills at school.

69 – perfecto | **perfect**

Este color de pintura es perfecto para el baño. | This paint color is perfect for the bathroom.
El clima está perfecto para ir de caminata. | The weather is perfect for going hiking.
¡Perfecto, justo lo que necesitaba! | Perfect, just what I needed!
Mi esposa es perfecta, la amo mucho. | My wife is perfect, I love her so much.
La casa será perfecta para nuestra familia. | The house will be perfect for our family.
Tu hermana es perfecta para ese trabajo. | Your sister is perfect for that job.
Los asientos son perfectos para ver el partido. | The seats are perfect to watch the game.
Estos jeans me quedan perfectos. | These jeans fit me perfectly.
Tus fotos quedaron perfectas con esa luz. | Your photos turned out perfect with that light.
Estas vacaciones estuvieron perfectas. | This vacation was perfect.

70 – sencillo — **simple, straightforward**

El menú es sencillo pero sabroso. — The menu is simple but tasty.
No es tan sencillo como parece. — It's not as simple as it seems.
Es muy sencillo, solo tienes que presionar este botón. — It's very simple, you just have to press this button.
Mi papá vive una vida sencilla en el campo. — My dad lives a simple life in the countryside.
La receta es sencilla, solo lleva tres ingredientes. — The recipe is simple, it only has three ingredients.
Dame una explicación sencilla. — Give me a simple explanation.
Quiero unos zapatos sencillos para diario. — I want some simple shoes for everyday use.
Prefiero métodos sencillos sin tantos pasos. — I prefer simple methods without so many steps.
La felicidad está en las cosas sencillas. — Happiness is in simple things.
Prefiero explicaciones sencillas y directas. — I prefer simple and direct explanations.

71 – lindo — **pretty, beautiful, nice, cute, lovely**

El pueblo es muy lindo en primavera. — The town is very pretty in spring.
Qué lindo bebé, parece un muñeco. — What a cute baby, he looks like a doll.
Pasamos un día lindo paseando por la ciudad. — We spent a lovely day strolling around the city.
Tienes una casa muy linda. — You have a very beautiful house.
Ella tiene una sonrisa linda. — She has a pretty smile.
Me gusta tu falda nueva, es muy linda. — I like your new skirt, it's very pretty.
Me gustan mucho tus aretes, son muy lindos. — I really like your earrings, they're very pretty.
¡Dios mío, tus gatitos son muy lindos! — My goodness, your kittens are so cute!
Las fotos de las vacaciones quedaron lindas. — The vacation photos turned out nice.
Tus nietas se ven lindas con esos vestidos. — Your granddaughters look pretty in those dresses.

72 – sucio — **dirty**

No quiero usar este baño sucio. — I don't want to use this dirty bathroom.
Lávate las manos después de tocar al perro sucio. — Wash your hands after touching the dirty dog.
No voy a nadar en este río sucio. — I won't swim in this dirty river.
Lavé mi ropa sucia. — I washed my dirty clothes.
El presidente tuvo una campaña sucia. — The president had a dirty campaign.
¿Por qué te sentaste en la silla sucia? — Why did you sit in the dirty chair?
Pon los platos sucios en el fregadero. — Put the dirty dishes in the sink.
¿Puedes ver a través de esas ventanas sucias? — Can you see through those dirty windows?
¿Qué quieres que haga con las toallas sucias? — What do you want me to do with the dirty towels?
Tus manos sucias dejaron marcas por todas partes. — Your dirty hands left marks everywhere.

73 – débil | **weak**

El equipo se ve débil esta temporada. | The team looks weak this season.
Mi abuelo está muy débil después de la operación. | My grandfather is very weak after the operation.
Tu argumento es débil, no me convence. | Your argument is weak, it doesn't convince me.
Mi abuela tiene la vista débil. | My grandmother has weak eyesight.
Mi mujer se sentía débil después del maratón. | My wife felt weak after the marathon.
La señal del wifi está débil en esa parte de la casa. | The wifi signal is weak in that part of the house.
Los argumentos de la defensa eran débiles. | The defense's arguments were weak.
Mis brazos están débiles después del gimnasio. | My arms are weak after the gym.
Estas plantas están débiles, necesitan más sol. | These plants are weak, they need more sun.
Mis piernas están débiles después de correr tanto. | My legs are weak after running so much.

74 – agradable | **pleasant, nice**

El clima hoy está muy agradable. | The weather today is very pleasant.
Es muy agradable conversar con ella. | It's very pleasant to talk with her.
El nuevo compañero de trabajo es muy agradable. | The new coworker is very nice.
Ella es muy agradable, les cae bien a todos. | She's very nice, everyone likes her.
La temperatura del agua está agradable para nadar. | The water temperature is pleasant for swimming.
Qué sorpresa tan agradable encontrarte aquí. | What a pleasant surprise to find you here.
Pasamos unos días agradables en la playa. | We spent some pleasant days at the beach.
Los vecinos nuevos son muy agradables. | The new neighbors are very nice.
Las temperaturas agradables me animan. | The pleasant temperatures cheer me up.
Fueron unas vacaciones agradables y relajantes. | It was a pleasant and relaxing vacation.

75 – cerrado | **closed**

El baño está cerrado, usa el de al lado. | The bathroom is closed, use the one next door.
Viven en un barrio cerrado. | They live in a gated community.
El restaurante está cerrado los lunes. | The restaurant is closed on Mondays.
La tienda ya estaba cerrada cuando llegamos. | The store was already closed when we arrived.
Ella tiene la mente cerrada a nuevas ideas. | She has a closed mind to new ideas.
La puerta estaba cerrada y no escuché nada. | The door was closed and I didn't hear anything.
Los bancos están cerrados los domingos. | The banks are closed on Sundays.
Estos pueblos son muy cerrados a los forasteros. | These towns are very closed off to outsiders.
Las mentes cerradas no aprenden cosas nuevas. | Closed minds don't learn new things.
Estas calles están cerradas al tráfico. | These streets are closed to traffic.

76 – ocupado	**busy, occupied**
Estoy muy ocupado con el trabajo esta semana.	I'm very busy with work this week.
El baño está ocupado.	The bathroom is occupied.
Este asiento está ocupado, ¿hay otro libre?	This seat is taken, is there another one free?
La doctora está ocupada con otro paciente.	The doctor is busy with another patient.
Mi tía está ocupada hablando con mi mamá.	My aunt is busy talking with my mom.
Ella está ocupada en una reunión muy larga.	She is busy in a very long meeting.
Mis abuelos están ocupados con el jardín.	My grandparents are busy with the garden.
Los niños están demasiado ocupados estos días.	Kids are too busy these days.
Todas las mesas están ocupadas en el restaurante.	All the tables are taken at the restaurant.
Las niñas están ocupadas haciendo la tarea.	The girls are busy doing homework.

77 – imposible	**impossible**
Es imposible llegar a tiempo con este tráfico.	It's impossible to arrive on time with this traffic.
Con ese calor es imposible dormir bien.	With that heat it's impossible to sleep well.
Ese examen estaba imposible, casi nadie lo pasó.	That exam was impossible, almost nobody passed it.
Es una tarea imposible de terminar en un día.	It's an impossible task to finish in one day.
Tu exigencia es imposible de aceptar.	Your demand is impossible to accept.
Ese tipo de comida es imposible de encontrar aquí.	That type of food is impossible to find here.
Nuestros horarios son imposibles de coordinar.	Our schedules are impossible to coordinate.
Los requisitos me parecieron imposibles.	The requirements seemed impossible to me.
Estas escaleras son imposibles con tacones.	These stairs are impossible with heels.
Esas metas son imposibles de alcanzar en un mes.	Those goals are impossible to reach in a month.

78 – lleno	**full**
El cine está lleno.	The movie theater is full.
Comí tanto que estoy lleno.	I ate so much that I'm full.
Mi celular está lleno de fotos.	My phone is full of photos.
Su vida está llena de aventuras.	Her life is full of adventures.
La tienda estaba llena en la mañana.	The store was packed in the morning.
La nevera está llena de comida.	The fridge is full of food.
Los restaurantes están llenos de turistas.	The restaurants are full of tourists.
Los buses están llenos a esta hora del día.	The buses are packed at this time of day.
Las calles están llenas de gente.	The streets are full of people.
Tengo las manos llenas.	I have my hands full.

79 – siguiente

next, following

Te veo el siguiente fin de semana. — I'll see you next weekend.
El siguiente paso es firmar el contrato. — The next step is to sign the contract.
Sigue derecho hasta el siguiente semáforo. — Keep going straight until the next traffic light.
Yo me bajo en la siguiente parada. — I'm getting off at the next stop.
Nos vemos la siguiente vez que vengas. — See you next time you come.
La siguiente semana tenemos vacaciones. — Next week we have vacation.
Lee los siguientes párrafos para mañana. — Read the following paragraphs for tomorrow.
En los siguientes días va a llover. — The next few days are going to rain.
Las siguientes instrucciones son importantes. — The following instructions are important.
En las siguientes horas habrá noticias. — There will be news in the next few hours.

80 – verdadero

real, true

Mi papá es un verdadero héroe para mí. — My dad is a true hero to me.
Este restaurante tiene verdadero sabor casero. — This restaurant has true homemade flavor.
Esta película es un verdadero clásico del cine. — This movie is a true classic of cinema.
Ella es una verdadera amiga. — She's a true friend.
Lo que pasó fue una verdadera tragedia. — What happened was a real tragedy.
¿Tienes una verdadera pasión en tu vida? — Do you have a true passion in your life?
Ellos son verdaderos profesionales en su trabajo. — They are true professionals in their work.
Mis padres son verdaderos modelos a seguir. — My parents are true role models.
¿Cuáles son tus verdaderas intenciones? — What are your true intentions?
Él nunca dijo las verdaderas razones. — He never said the real reasons.

81 – vivo

alive, lively, bright, vivid

¿Tu abuelo sigue vivo? — Is your grandfather still alive?
El coral vivo es frágil y debemos protegerlo. — Living coral is fragile and we must protect it.
Todo ser vivo necesita oxígeno para sobrevivir. — Every living being needs oxygen to survive.
Me encanta esa blusa de color rosa vivo. — I love that bright pink blouse.
La imagen viva de ese recuerdo nunca se me olvida. — The vivid image of that memory never leaves me.
La esperanza está viva en sus corazones. — Hope is alive in their hearts.
Prefiero ropa con colores vivos. — I prefer clothes with bright colors.
Los colores vivos estaban de moda en los ochenta. — Bright colors were trendy in the eighties.
Las tradiciones mexicanas siguen vivas. — Mexican traditions remain alive.
Las lenguas vivas evolucionan constantemente. — Living languages constantly evolve.

82 – excelente | **excellent**

El clima está excelente para ir a la playa. | The weather is excellent for going to the beach.
Tu hijo es un estudiante excelente. | Your son is an excellent student.
Ese restaurante tiene un excelente servicio. | That restaurant has excellent service.
Esa es una excelente idea. | That's an excellent idea.
Fue una excelente decisión mudarnos acá. | It was an excellent decision for us to move here.
La profesora nueva es excelente. | The new teacher is excellent.
La película recibió excelentes comentarios. | The movie got excellent reviews.
Estos tacos están excelentes. | These tacos are excellent.
Tus calificaciones son excelentes este semestre. | Your grades are excellent this semester.
Las empanadas quedaron excelentes. | The empanadas turned out excellent.

83 – guapo | **handsome, good-looking, pretty**

El actor de esa película es guapo. | The actor in that movie is handsome.
Tu novio es muy guapo, tienes suerte. | Your boyfriend is really handsome, you're lucky.
Mi papá era guapo cuando era joven. | My dad was handsome when he was young.
Te ves guapa con ese vestido. | You look so pretty in that dress.
¿Conoces a la chica guapa del segundo piso? | Do you know the pretty girl from the second floor?
La actriz se ve guapa con el cabello corto. | The actress looks pretty with short hair.
Todos los chicos de esa banda son guapos. | All the guys in that band are handsome.
Se ven guapos en la foto de grupo. | They look handsome in the group picture.
Las bailarinas se ven guapas en el escenario. | The dancers look pretty on stage.
Tus primas están cada vez más guapas. | Your cousins are getting prettier and prettier.

84 – muerto | **dead**

Mi abuelo está muerto desde hace dos años. | My grandfather has been dead for two years.
Llegué muerto del trabajo anoche. | I came home dead tired from work last night.
Este pueblo está muerto los domingos. | This town is dead on Sundays.
La batería del carro está muerta. | The car battery is dead.
La planta está muerta por falta de agua. | The plant is dead from lack of water.
La fiesta estaba muerta hasta que llegamos. | The party was dead until we arrived.
Todos mis abuelos están muertos. | All of my grandparents are dead.
Hay muchos soldados muertos a causa de la guerra. | There are many dead soldiers because of the war.
Las calles están muertas a esta hora. | The streets are dead at this hour.
Las flores están muertas por el calor. | The flowers are dead from the heat.

85 – típico
El mariachi es un símbolo típico de la cultura mexicana.
Un frío intenso es típico en enero aquí.
Ese es un comportamiento típico de los adolescentes.
La comida típica de aquí es deliciosa.
La cumbia es música típica que bailamos en las fiestas.
Es la típica historia de amor que termina mal.
Las empanadas son una comida típica de Argentina.
Los tacos son platillos típicos de México.
Son problemas típicos de las grandes ciudades.
Las arepas son preparaciones típicas de Colombia.

typical
Mariachi is a typical symbol of Mexican culture.
Intense cold is typical here in January.
That's typical behavior of teenagers.
The typical food from here is delicious.
Cumbia is typical music we dance to at parties.
It's the typical love story that ends badly.
Empanadas are typical foods from Argentina.
Tacos are typical dishes from Mexico.
They're typical problems of big cities.
Arepas are typical preparations from Colombia.

86 – corto
El vestido te queda muy corto.
Fue un viaje corto pero increíble.
Me corté el cabello demasiado corto esta vez.
La película fue corta pero muy buena.
La reunión fue corta.
Esta falda es demasiado corta para la oficina.
Prefiero los cuentos cortos a las novelas largas.
Los días son más cortos en invierno.
Las mangas de esta chaqueta son cortas.
Las faldas cortas están de moda este año.

short
The dress is too short on you.
It was a short but incredible trip.
I cut my hair too short this time.
The movie was short but very good.
The meeting was short.
This skirt is too short for the office.
I prefer short stories to long novels.
The days are shorter in winter.
The sleeves of this jacket are short.
Short skirts are in fashion this year.

87 – vacío
¿De quién es el vaso vacío que está en la mesa?
Compré un terreno vacío para construir mi casa.
Traigo el tanque vacío, necesito llenarlo.
La casa se siente vacía sin los niños.
La piscina vacía se llenó de hojas secas.
Una promesa vacía no vale nada.
Los parques estaban vacíos por la lluvia.
El bar está lleno de vasos vacíos.
Tira esas cajas vacías.
Tus amenazas vacías no me afectan.

empty
Whose empty glass is on the table?
I bought an empty lot to build my house.
I've got an empty gas tank, I need to fill it up.
The house feels empty without the kids.
The empty pool filled up with dry leaves.
An empty promise is worth nothing.
The parks were empty because of the rain.
The bar is full of empty glasses.
Throw out those empty boxes.
Your empty threats don't affect me.

88 – rojo

red

¿El carro rojo es tuyo? — Is the red car yours?
El semáforo rojo significa alto. — The red light means stop.
¿La bandera de tu país tiene rojo? — Does your country's flag have red in it?
La salsa roja pica mucho. — The red sauce is very spicy.
Compré una rosa roja para mi mamá. — I bought a red rose for my mom.
Tu cara está toda roja por el sol. — Your face is all red from the sun.
Los ojos rojos son una señal de cansancio. — Red eyes are a sign of tiredness.
Los tomates rojos ya están listos. — The red tomatoes are ready now.
Mis mejillas están rojas de vergüenza. — My cheeks are red from embarrassment.
Compré unas manzanas rojas en el mercado. — I bought some red apples at the market.

89 – azul

blue

Un carro azul está estacionado frente a mi casa. — A blue car is parked in front of my house.
El cielo está completamente azul hoy. — The sky is completely blue today.
El uniforme azul del colegio es obligatorio. — The blue school uniform is mandatory.
Esa falda azul combina perfecto con tus zapatos. — That blue skirt matches perfectly with your shoes.
La puerta de entrada de mi casa es azul. — The front door of my house is blue.
La luz azul es mala para dormir. — Blue light is bad for sleep.
Los peces azules del acuario son mis favoritos. — The blue fish in the aquarium are my favorites.
Se usaron los globos azules para decorar la fiesta. — The blue balloons were used to decorate the party.
Compré unas toallas azules para el baño. — I bought some blue towels for the bathroom.
Mis tazas favoritas son las azules. — My favorite cups are the blue ones.

90 – antiguo

old, ancient, former, antique

Compré un reloj antiguo en el mercado de pulgas. — I bought an antique watch at the flea market.
Este edificio antiguo tiene más de doscientos años. — This old building is over two hundred years old.
El carro antiguo de mi papá todavía funciona. — My dad's old car still works.
El antiguo presidente visitó la ciudad ayer. — The former president visited the city yesterday.
Mi antigua jefa me recomendó. — My former boss recommended me.
La tradición antigua se mantiene en mi familia. — The old tradition is maintained in my family.
Los métodos antiguos a veces son mejores. — The old methods are sometimes better.
Compramos muebles antiguos en la subasta. — We bought antique furniture at the auction.
Las recetas antiguas de mi abuela son deliciosas. — My grandmother's old recipes are delicious.
Las ruinas antiguas atraen a muchos turistas. — The ancient ruins attract many tourists.

91 – dulce

El té sabe dulce. ¿Le pusiste miel?
Me mandó un mensaje tan dulce que casi lloro.
El niño tiene un carácter dulce y tranquilo.
Su mirada era dulce pero triste al mismo tiempo.
Tiene una sonrisa dulce que conquista a todos.
Me encanta la piña cuando está bien dulce.
Estos caramelos son demasiado dulces para mí.
Los postres dulces son mi debilidad.
Las manzanas son sorprendentemente dulces.
Las uvas están en su punto, bien dulces.

sweet

The tea tastes sweet. Did you add honey?
He sent me such a sweet message I almost cried.
The boy has a sweet and calm personality.
Her gaze was sweet but sad at the same time.
She has a sweet smile that wins everyone over.
I love pineapple when it's really sweet.
These candies are too sweet for me.
Sweet desserts are my weakness.
The apples are surprisingly sweet.
The grapes are just right, really sweet.

92 – loco

Estás loco, me haces reír mucho.
Estoy loco por ti.
Me vuelve loco cuando no me contesta.
La fiesta estuvo loca.
Sé que mi idea es loca, pero hagámoslo.
Mi abuela está medio loca, pero la queremos.
Los chicos están locos por esa chica nueva.
Los precios están locos en este lugar.
Las cosas están muy locas en el trabajo.
Las chicas están locas por ese cantante.

crazy

You're crazy, you make me laugh a lot.
I'm crazy about you.
It drives me crazy when he doesn't answer me.
The party was wild.
I know my idea is crazy, but let's do it.
My grandma is a bit crazy, but we love her.
The guys are crazy about that new girl.
The prices are crazy in this place.
Things are really crazy at work.
The girls are crazy about that singer.

93 – correcto

¿Me puedes decir si esto es correcto?
No creo que ese sea el camino correcto.
El pronóstico del tiempo resultó correcto.
¿Esta información es correcta?
No tengo la dirección correcta de su casa.
Esa no es la decisión correcta en este caso.
Estos números no me parecen correctos.
Sus modales son muy correctos.
Las medidas que tomaste son correctas.
Sus respuestas fueron todas correctas.

correct, right

Can you tell me if this is right?
I don't think that's the right path.
The weather forecast turned out to be correct.
Is this information correct?
I don't have the correct address for his house.
That's not the right decision in this case.
These numbers don't seem correct to me.
His manners are very proper.
The measurements you took are correct.
Her answers were all correct.

94 – lento | **slow**

Mi carro es lento pero confiable. | My car is slow but reliable.
El ascensor es tan lento que prefiero las escaleras. | The elevator is so slow that I prefer the stairs.
¿Por qué mi internet está tan lento hoy? | Why is my internet so slow today?
La computadora vieja es muy lenta. | The old computer is very slow.
La cola en la tienda estaba lenta. | The line at the store was slow.
La música lenta me relaja mucho. | Slow music relaxes me a lot.
Los cambios han sido lentos pero constantes. | The changes have been slow but steady.
Los perezosos son más lentos que las tortugas. | Sloths are slower than turtles.
Mis hijas son muy lentas en las mañanas. | My girls are really slow in the mornings.
Las descargas están lentas hoy. | Downloads are slow today.

95 – simpático | **nice, friendly**

Ese chico es simpático, me cae bien. | That guy is nice, I like him.
Ese doctor es muy simpático con los niños. | That doctor is really nice with kids.
El chico nuevo del trabajo es simpático. | The new guy at work is nice.
La vecina nueva parece simpática. | The new neighbor seems friendly.
La doctora es muy simpática. | The doctor is very friendly.
La cajera fue simpática conmigo. | The cashier was friendly with me.
Los meseros de ese restaurante son simpáticos. | The waiters at that restaurant are friendly.
Mis suegros son simpáticos. | My in-laws are nice.
Esas señoras simpáticas nos ofrecieron café. | Those nice ladies offered us coffee.
Las profesoras son simpáticas con los niños. | The teachers are nice with the kids.

96 – enorme | **enormous, huge**

El perro de mi vecino es enorme. | My neighbor's dog is huge.
Tengo un enorme respeto por mi abuela. | I have enormous respect for my grandmother.
El parque tiene un árbol enorme en el centro. | The park has a huge tree in the middle.
Cometí un error enorme. | I made an enormous mistake.
Fue una sorpresa enorme recibir ese regalo. | It was a huge surprise to get that gift.
Sentí una alegría enorme cuando los vi. | I felt enormous joy when I saw them.
Esos árboles enormes dan mucha sombra. | Those enormous trees give a lot of shade.
Los niños son una enorme responsabilidad. | Children are an enormous responsibility.
Las filas para entrar al concierto eran enormes. | The lines to get into the concert were enormous.
Las enormes olas del mar asustaron a los turistas. | The enormous ocean waves scared the tourists.

97 – increíble
Ese gol fue increíble.
Te ves increíble con ese traje nuevo.
Ese truco de magia fue increíble.
Es increíble la cantidad de gente que vino.
La energía en el estadio era increíble.
Tu paciencia con los niños es increíble.
Los efectos especiales de la película son increíbles.
Esos tacos están increíbles, pruébalos.
Las playas de México son increíbles.
Las vacaciones estuvieron increíbles.

incredible
That goal was incredible.
You look incredible in that new suit.
That magic trick was incredible.
The amount of people who came is incredible.
The energy in the stadium was incredible.
Your patience with children is incredible.
The special effects in the movie are incredible.
Those tacos are incredible, try them.
The beaches in Mexico are incredible.
The vacation was incredible.

98 – contento
Estoy contento con mi nuevo trabajo.
El niño está contento jugando en el parque.
Mi papá está contento con el regalo que le dimos.
Mi hija está contenta en su nuevo colegio.
Quedó muy contenta con su corte de pelo.
María se ve muy contenta desde que se casó.
Mis abuelos estaban contentos de vernos.
Todos estamos contentos de estar aquí reunidos.
Las chicas estaban contentas con las fotos.
Las niñas están contentas con sus regalos.

happy, pleased, satisfied
I'm happy with my new job.
The boy is happy playing in the park.
My dad is pleased with the gift we gave him.
My daughter is happy at her new school.
She was really pleased with her haircut.
María looks very happy since she got married.
My grandparents were happy to see us.
We're all happy to be here gathered together.
The girls were happy with the pictures.
The girls are happy with their gifts.

99 – moderno
Me encanta el diseño moderno de la cocina.
El arte moderno a veces es difícil de entender.
El hospital moderno está bien equipado.
Mi mamá quiere una cocina moderna con isla.
La decoración del hotel es moderna y sencilla.
La tecnología moderna facilita la vida.
Los edificios modernos dominan el centro.
Los edificios modernos no tienen ningún encanto.
Las casas modernas suelen tener ventanas grandes.
Esas sillas modernas son bonitas pero incómodas.

modern
I love the modern design of the kitchen.
Modern art is sometimes hard to understand.
The modern hospital is well equipped.
My mom wants a modern kitchen with an island.
The hotel's decoration is modern and simple.
Modern technology makes life easier.
Modern buildings dominate downtown.
Modern buildings don't have any charm.
Modern houses usually have large windows.
Those modern chairs are pretty but uncomfortable.

100 – temprano

early

El café temprano es parte de mi rutina diaria.
Early coffee is part of my daily routine.

Mi vuelo temprano sale a las seis y media.
My early flight leaves at six thirty.

El turno temprano empieza a las seis.
The early shift starts at six.

La reunión temprana fue cancelada por el jefe.
The early meeting was canceled by the boss.

La detección temprana del cáncer es importante.
Early detection of cancer is important.

Una cena temprana nos ayuda a dormir mejor.
An early dinner helps us sleep better.

Los horarios tempranos no son para todos.
Early schedules aren't for everyone.

Los vuelos tempranos suelen ser más baratos.
Early flights are usually cheaper.

Las clases tempranas siempre están vacías.
Early classes are always empty.

Las horas tempranas del día son tranquilas.
The early hours of the day are peaceful.

101 – famoso

famous

Messi es un famoso jugador de fútbol.
Messi is a famous soccer player.

El lugar es famoso por su comida típica.
The place is famous for its traditional food.

Mi hermano es famoso por llegar tarde a todo.
My brother is famous for being late to everything.

Esta playa es famosa por sus aguas cristalinas.
This beach is famous for its crystal-clear waters.

Mi prima quiere ser una actriz famosa.
My cousin wants to be a famous actress.

Esa playa es famosa por sus atardeceres.
That beach is famous for its sunsets.

Los mariachis más famosos tocan en la plaza.
The most famous mariachis play in the plaza.

Los actores famosos cobran millones por película.
Famous actors charge millions per movie.

Las hermanas famosas lanzaron su propia marca.
The famous sisters launched their own brand.

Las actrices famosas llegaron a la alfombra roja.
The famous actresses arrived at the red carpet.

102 – cómodo

comfortable, convenient

Este sillón es cómodo para ver televisión.
This armchair is comfortable for watching TV.

Me siento más cómodo hablando en privado.
I feel more comfortable talking in private.

El horario de trabajo es bastante cómodo.
The work schedule is quite convenient.

Esta cama es muy cómoda, dormí perfectamente.
This bed is very comfortable, I slept perfectly.

La silla de la oficina no es nada cómoda.
The office chair isn't comfortable at all.

La temperatura está bastante cómoda aquí adentro.
The temperature is quite comfortable in here.

Los muebles de la sala son bastante cómodos.
The living room furniture is quite comfortable.

Estos zapatos son cómodos pero feos.
These shoes are comfortable but ugly.

Las almohadas del hotel no son nada cómodas.
The hotel pillows aren't comfortable at all.

Estas medias son más cómodas que esas.
These socks are more comfortable than those.

103 – complicado
Este plato es complicado de preparar.
Mi padre es un hombre complicado de entender.
Este juego es más complicado de lo que parece.
Es una receta complicada, pero vale la pena.
La tarea de química de hoy está complicada.
La situación en el trabajo está complicada.
Los trámites para sacar la visa son complicados.
Los videojuegos de ahora son complicados.
Las reglas del juego son complicadas.
Las cosas se pusieron complicadas en la oficina.

complicated
This dish is complicated to prepare.
My father is a complicated man to understand.
This game is more complicated than it looks.
It's a complicated recipe, but it's worth it.
Today's chemistry homework is complicated.
The situation at work is complicated.
The procedures to get the visa are complicated.
Video games nowadays are complicated.
The rules of the game are complicated.
Things got complicated at the office.

104 – distinto
El acento de esta región es bastante distinto.
Mi estilo de cocinar es muy distinto al tuyo.
Cada especie tiene un comportamiento distinto.
Cada profesor tiene una metodología distinta.
Su reacción fue completamente distinta a la mía.
Esta versión es distinta a la original.
Son estilos de vida completamente distintos.
Los precios son distintos en cada supermercado.
Las tradiciones de cada pueblo son distintas.
Las costumbres son distintas en cada familia.

distinct, different
This region's accent is quite distinct.
My cooking style is very distinct from yours.
Each species has distinct behavior.
Each teacher has a distinct methodology.
Her reaction was completely different from mine.
This version is different from the original.
They're completely distinct lifestyles.
The prices are different in each supermarket.
Each town's traditions are distinct.
The customs are different in each family.

105 – práctico
Necesito un regalo práctico para mi papá.
Este carro es muy práctico para la ciudad.
Es un regalo práctico, todos lo pueden usar.
Esta mochila es muy práctica para viajar.
Una linterna es práctica en un apagón.
Su experiencia práctica la ayudó mucho.
Estos zapatos son prácticos para caminar mucho.
Los cursos prácticos me ayudan más que la teoría.
Tus ideas son prácticas y fáciles de aplicar.
Necesito soluciones prácticas, no complicadas.

practical
I need a practical gift for my dad.
This car is very practical for the city.
It's a practical gift, everyone can use it.
This backpack is very practical for traveling.
A flashlight is practical during a blackout.
Her practical experience helped her a lot.
These shoes are practical for walking a lot.
Practical courses help me more than theory.
Your ideas are practical and easy to apply.
I need practical solutions, not complicated ones.

106 – peligroso | **dangerous**

Manejar tan rápido es peligroso. | Driving that fast is dangerous.
Ese barrio es peligroso de noche. | That neighborhood is dangerous at night.
Es peligroso caminar solo por ahí. | It's dangerous to walk alone around there.
La fiebre alta es peligrosa para los bebés. | High fever is dangerous for babies.
La bacteria Salmonella es peligrosa si se ingiere. | Salmonella bacteria is dangerous if ingested.
La situación se está volviendo peligrosa. | The situation is getting dangerous.
Los rayos del sol son peligrosos. | The sun's rays are dangerous.
Los perros callejeros a veces son peligrosos. | Stray dogs are sometimes dangerous.
Las armas son peligrosas en manos de niños. | Guns are dangerous in children's hands.
Las drogas son muy peligrosas. | Drugs are very dangerous.

107 – amarillo | **yellow**

Vi un pajaro amarillo en el jardín esta mañana. | I saw a yellow bird in the garden this morning.
El plátano ya está amarillo, listo para comerse. | The banana is yellow now, ready to be eaten.
El amarillo era el color favorito de mi abuela. | Yellow was my grandmother's favorite color.
La casa amarilla de la esquina está en venta. | The yellow house on the corner is for sale.
Me encanta la blusa amarilla que tienes puesta. | I love the yellow blouse you're wearing.
La luz amarilla del semáforo significa precaución. | The yellow traffic light means caution.
Los autobuses amarillos llevan a los niños al colegio. | The yellow buses take the children to school.
Los pimientos amarillos están en oferta. | The yellow peppers are on sale.
Compré unas servilletas amarillas para la fiesta. | I bought some yellow napkins for the party.
Las luces amarillas del semáforo parpadeaban. | The yellow lights on the traffic signal were flashing.

108 – básico | **basic**

Es un error básico de principiantes. | It's a basic beginners' mistake.
Es un modelo básico de celular, pero funciona bien. | It's a basic cell phone model, but it works fine.
El curso es muy básico. | The course is very basic.
Mi abuela preparó una comida básica pero deliciosa. | My grandmother prepared a basic but delicious meal.
Esta receta es muy básica y fácil de preparar. | This recipe is very basic and easy to prepare.
La versión básica no tiene muchas funciones. | The basic version doesn't have many features.
Los ingredientes básicos son harina, agua y sal. | The basic ingredients are flour, water and salt.
Estos son los conceptos básicos que debes aprender. | These are the basic concepts you should learn.
Las necesidades básicas incluyen comida y vivienda. | Basic needs include food and housing.
Aprendí técnicas básicas viendo a mi mamá. | I learned basic techniques watching my mom.

109 – menor | **younger, smaller**

Mi hermano menor todavía vive en casa. | My younger brother still lives at home.
Este problema es menor comparado con el otro. | This problem is minor compared to the other one.
El riesgo es menor de lo que parece. | The risk is smaller than it seems.
La diferencia es menor de lo esperado. | The difference is smaller than expected.
No tengo la menor duda. | I don't have the slightest doubt.
La distancia es menor por esta vía. | The distance is shorter this way.
Mis hijos menores todavía van a la primaria. | My younger kids still go to elementary school.
Tuvieron daños menores en la casa. | They had minor damage in the house.
Las pérdidas menores no afectan al negocio. | The minor losses don't affect the business.
Las hijas menores se parecen mucho. | The younger daughters look a lot alike.

110 – suficiente | **enough, sufficient**

No tuve suficiente tiempo para terminar. | I didn't have enough time to finish.
¿Hay suficiente arroz para todos? | Is there enough rice for everyone?
No tengo suficiente dinero para comprar el celular. | I don't have enough money to buy the phone.
La explicación fue suficiente para entender. | The explanation was enough to understand.
No hay suficiente agua caliente para todos. | There isn't enough hot water for everyone.
No tengo suficiente paciencia para ser profesor. | I don't have enough patience to be a teacher.
Ya tenemos suficientes problemas. | We already have enough problems.
No tenemos suficientes datos para decidir. | We don't have enough data to decide.
¿Hay suficientes sillas para todos? | Are there enough chairs for everyone?
¿Trajiste suficientes bolsas para las compras? | Did you bring enough bags for the groceries?

111 – peor | **worse, worst**

El clima está peor en invierno. | The weather is worse in winter.
Ese fue el peor error de mi vida. | That was the worst mistake of my life.
Mi dolor de espalda está peor. | My back pain is worse.
La situación está peor de lo que creíamos. | The situation is worse than we thought.
La película estuvo peor de lo que imaginaba. | The movie was worse than I imagined.
La noticia fue peor de lo que esperaba. | The news was worse than I expected.
Mi papá cuenta los peores chistes. | My dad tells the worst jokes.
Él siempre imagina los peores escenarios. | He always imagines the worst scenarios.
Mis calificaciones son peores este año. | My grades are worse this year.
Tomo las peores decisiones cuando estoy cansado. | I make the worst decisions when I'm tired.

112 – entero | **whole, entire**

Me comí el pastel entero yo solo. | I ate the whole cake by myself.
Pasamos el día entero en la playa. | We spent the whole day at the beach.
El pueblo entero salió a celebrar. | The whole town came out to celebrate.
Se pasó la noche entera estudiando. | She spent the whole night studying.
La familia entera vino a la boda. | The entire family came to the wedding.
Leí la novela entera en dos días. | I read the entire novel in two days.
Pasamos dos días enteros en la carretera. | We spent two whole days on the road.
Vendemos pescados enteros en el mercado. | We sell whole fish at the market.
Pasaron tardes enteras jugando videojuegos. | They spent entire afternoons playing video games.
Se quedaron dos semanas enteras sin internet. | They went two whole weeks without internet.

113 – justo | **fair, right, just**

Es un castigo justo por lo que hizo. | It's a fair punishment for what he did.
El precio me parece justo para ese trabajo. | The price seems fair to me for that job.
Él llegó justo cuando empezaba la película. | He arrived just when the movie was starting.
La división de la herencia fue justa. | The division of the inheritance was fair.
Ella trata de ser justa con todos. | She tries to be fair with everyone.
Esa crítica me parece justa. | That criticism seems fair to me.
Los árbitros fueron justos en el torneo. | The referees were fair in the tournament.
Los salarios justos son importantes para la sociedad. | Fair wages are important for society.
Las reglas son justas para ambos equipos. | The rules are fair for both teams.
Sus decisiones siempre han sido justas. | Her decisions have always been fair.

114 – equivocado | **wrong, mistaken**

Creo que estás equivocado. | I think you're wrong.
Yo estaba equivocado desde el principio. | I was wrong from the start.
El diagnóstico resultó estar equivocado. | The diagnosis turned out to be wrong.
La dirección que me dieron está equivocada. | The address they gave me is wrong.
Esa respuesta está completamente equivocada. | That answer is completely wrong.
Creo que tu impresión sobre ella es equivocada. | I think your impression of her is wrong.
Ustedes están equivocados con esa idea. | You all are wrong with that idea.
Todos pensábamos igual, pero estábamos equivocados. | We all thought the same, but we were wrong.
Creo que nuestras suposiciones están equivocadas. | I think our assumptions are wrong.
Todas mis predicciones estaban equivocadas. | All my predictions were wrong.

115 – reciente | **recent**
El cambio reciente en la ley generó debate. | The recent change in the law sparked debate.
Su trabajo reciente recibió buenas críticas. | His recent work got good reviews.
¿Es este un cambio reciente en la norma? | Is this a recent change to the rule?
Esa decisión reciente fue muy polémica. | That recent decision was very controversial.
Su reciente llegada al equipo mejoró todo. | His recent arrival to the team improved everything.
Es una película reciente, salió hace dos semanas. | It's a recent movie, it came out two weeks ago.
¿Leíste los mensajes recientes del grupo? | Did you read the recent messages from the group?
Los eventos recientes han sido muy estresantes. | Recent events have been very stressful.
Las noticias recientes son desalentadoras. | The recent news is discouraging.
Las estadísticas recientes muestran una mejoría. | The recent statistics show an improvement.

116 – extraño | **strange**
Es extraño estar en esta casa sin mis padres. | It's strange being in this house without my parents.
Me parece extraño que él no haya venido. | It seems strange to me that he didn't come.
Es un sabor extraño, pero rico. | It's a strange taste, but tasty.
Ella tiene una manera extraña de hablar. | She has a strange way of speaking.
La situación es bastante extraña. | The situation is pretty strange.
Ella me lanzó una mirada extraña. | She gave me a strange look.
Han pasado eventos muy extraños aquí. | Very strange events have happened here.
Él me contó unos sueños extraños. | He told me about some strange dreams.
Escuchamos voces extrañas afuera. | We heard strange voices outside.
Esas ideas extrañas no van a funcionar. | Those weird ideas aren't going to work.

117 – tonto | **stupid, silly, dumb**
Fue un error tonto. | It was a dumb mistake.
No seas tonto. | Don't be silly.
Es un programa tonto, pero me hace reír. | This is a silly show, but it makes me laugh.
Qué pregunta más tonta. | What a dumb question.
Esa película es medio tonta pero me gusta. | That movie is kind of dumb, but I like it.
Esa canción tonta se me pegó todo el día. | That silly song got stuck in my head all day.
Compré esta cosa tonta y no sirve para nada. | I bought this dumb thing and it's useless.
Tus planes tontos nunca funcionarán. | Your foolish plans will never work.
Compartimos bromas tontas que nadie más entiende. | We share silly jokes that nobody else understands.
Tomamos muchas fotos tontas. | We took a lot of silly photos.

118 – duro | **tough, hard**

Este pan está duro, ya no sirve. | This bread is hard, it's no good anymore.
Me pegó duro la noticia. | The news hit me hard.
Fue un día duro en el trabajo. | It was a tough day at work.
Esta cama es demasiado dura para mí. | This bed is too hard for me.
La carne está muy dura. | The meat is very tough.
La vida es dura, pero tú sigue adelante. | Life is hard, but you keep going.
Esos señores son duros para negociar. | Those guys are tough to negotiate with.
Los tiempos son duros. | Times are tough.
Las condiciones de trabajo eran duras. | The working conditions were tough.
Pasamos por unas semanas duras. | We went through some hard weeks.

119 – falso | **false, fake**

Ella me dio un número falso. | She gave me a fake number.
No creas ese rumor falso. | Don't believe that false rumor.
Mi reloj resultó ser falso. | My watch turned out to be fake.
La información que te dieron es falsa. | The information they gave you is false.
La falsa alarma nos asustó a todos. | The false alarm scared all of us.
Esa cartera es una imitación falsa. | That purse is a fake imitation.
Vendían productos falsos en el mercado. | They were selling fake products at the market.
Todos los perfiles falsos fueron borrados. | All the fake profiles were deleted.
Las acusaciones contra él son falsas. | The accusations against him are false.
Hay muchas noticias falsas en internet. | There is a lot of fake news on the internet.

120 – pesado | **heavy**

Este bolso está muy pesado. | This bag is really heavy.
El tráfico está pesado esta mañana. | Traffic is heavy this morning.
El almuerzo estuvo pesado, y me dio sueño. | Lunch was heavy, and it made me sleepy.
La mochila está pesada con todos los libros. | The backpack is heavy with all the books.
La cena estuvo pesada, mejor no como postre. | Dinner was heavy, I better not have dessert.
La caja es demasiado pesada para moverla tú sola. | The box is too heavy to move by yourself.
Los muebles son demasiado pesados para moverlos tú solo. | The furniture is too heavy to move alone.
Los platos tradicionales son pesados pero sabrosos. | Traditional dishes are heavy but tasty.
Las bolsas del súper están pesadas. | The grocery bags are heavy.
Las comidas pesadas no me caen bien en la noche. | Heavy meals don't sit well with me at night.

121 – raro — **weird, strange**

Es un tipo raro. — He's a weird guy.
Él tiene un sentido del humor raro. — He has a weird sense of humor.
Está pasando algo raro. — Something weird is going on.
Mi novia es un poco rara, pero la amo. — My girlfriend is a little strange, but I love her.
Qué rara coincidencia. — What a strange coincidence.
Esta leche sabe rara, mejor no la tomes. — This milk tastes weird, better not drink it.
Los vecinos nuevos son raros. — The new neighbors are weird.
También tienen algunos hijos raros. — They have some weird kids, too.
Todas las chicas de ese club son raras. — Every girl in that club is weird.
Hacen cosas raras. — They do weird things.

122 – caliente — **hot**

¡El agua está caliente! Me quemé. — The water is hot! I burned myself.
El motor del carro está caliente después del viaje. — The car engine is hot after the trip.
No toques la sartén, está caliente. — Don't touch the pan, it's hot.
No puedo dormir con la habitación tan caliente. — I can't sleep with the room so hot.
La arena está caliente, ponte sandalias. — The sand is hot, put on sandals.
La sopa está caliente, sóplale un poco. — The soup is hot, blow on it a little.
Los tamales están calientes, recién hechos. — The tamales are hot, just made.
¿Las papas fritas todavía están calientes? — Are the french fries still hot?
Las toallas están calientes por la secadora. — The towels are hot from the dryer.
Las empanadas estaban calientes y deliciosas. — The empanadas were hot and delicious.

123 – positivo — **positive**

Trato de ver el lado positivo de todo. — I try to see the positive side of everything.
El resultado del examen de gripe salió positivo. — The result of the flu test came out positive.
Ese cambio tuvo un efecto positivo en mi vida. — That change had a positive effect on my life.
Me gusta rodearme de gente positiva. — I like to surround myself with positive people.
Ella siempre tiene una actitud positiva. — She always has a positive attitude.
Su actitud positiva contagia a todos. — Her positive attitude is contagious to everyone.
Los resultados del examen salieron positivos. — The test results came out positive.
Están haciendo cambios positivos en la comunidad. — They're making positive changes in the community.
Esas palabras positivas me dieron confianza. — Those positive words gave me confidence.
Las críticas han sido mayormente positivas. — The reviews have been mostly positive.

124 – negativo | **negative**

El resultado del examen salió negativo. | The test result came out negative.
Ese hábito tiene un efecto negativo en tu salud. | That habit has a negative effect on your health.
El diagnóstico médico resultó negativo, por suerte. | The medical diagnosis turned out negative, luckily.
Él recibió una crítica muy negativa del jefe. | He received very negative criticism from the boss.
La actitud de Ana ha sido muy negativa últimamente. | Ana's attitude has been very negative lately.
Su actitud negativa afecta a todo el equipo. | Her negative attitude affects the whole team.
Sus comentarios negativos no ayudan en nada. | His negative comments don't help at all.
Los efectos negativos de fumar son claros. | The negative effects of smoking are clear.
Las críticas negativas no la desanimaron. | The negative criticisms didn't discourage her.
Es difícil evitar las noticias negativas. | It's hard to avoid negative news.

125 – fresco | **fresh, cool**

Este jugo sabe fresco. | This juice tastes fresh.
El pescado que vendemos es muy fresco. | The fish we sell is very fresh.
El aire fresco de la mañana me despierta. | The fresh morning air wakes me up.
La pintura aún está fresca. | The paint is still fresh.
La brisa fresca entra por la ventana. | The cool breeze comes through the window.
La fruta fresca es más sabrosa. | Fresh fruit is more flavorful.
Estos tomates son de mi huerto, están frescos. | These tomatoes are from my garden, they're fresh.
Venden mariscos frescos en el mercado. | They sell fresh seafood at the market.
Las noches frescas son perfectas para dormir. | Cool nights are perfect for sleeping.
Las verduras frescas son más nutritivas. | Fresh vegetables are more nutritious.

126 – ligero | **light**

Este paquete es tan ligero que parece vacío. | This package is so light that it seems empty.
Tomé un desayuno ligero antes del gimnasio. | I had a light breakfast before the gym.
Tengo el sueño ligero. | I'm a light sleeper.
Su maleta es más ligera de lo que esperaba. | Your suitcase is lighter than I expected.
Está fresco afuera, así que trae una chaqueta ligera. | It's cool out, so bring a light jacket.
Esta noche solo quiero una cena ligera. | Tonight I want only a light dinner.
Estos zapatos ligeros son perfectos para correr. | These light shoes are great for running.
Los niños pequeños tienen pasos muy ligeros. | Little children have such light footsteps.
Estas cajas están ligeras, las puedo cargar. | These boxes are light, I can carry them.
Compré blusas ligeras para el verano. | I bought lightweight blouses for summer.

127 – seco | **dry**

El clima aquí es seco todo el año. | The climate here is dry all year round.
Prefiero el vino seco, no el vino dulce. | I prefer dry wine, not sweet wine.
El pollo siempre me queda seco. | My chicken always turns out dry.
Toma agua si tienes la garganta seca. | Drink water if your throat is dry.
¿Ya está seca la ropa? | Are the clothes dry yet?
La tierra está seca porque no ha llovido en semanas. | The soil is dry because it hasn't rained in weeks.
Los chiles secos son para el mole. | The dried chiles are for the mole.
Los árboles están secos por falta de lluvia. | The trees are dry from lack of rain.
Las hojas secas crujen al pisarse. | The dry leaves crunch when stepped on.
Tengo las manos secas, necesito crema. | My hands are dry, I need some lotion.

128 – atractivo | **attractive, appealing**

Ese chico es muy atractivo, todas hablan de él. | That guy is very attractive, everyone talks about him.
El salario no es tan atractivo como esperaba. | The salary isn't as attractive as I expected.
El paquete a Cancún suena atractivo. | The package to Cancún sounds appealing.
Esa actriz colombiana es súper atractiva. | That Colombian actress is super attractive.
La idea de estudiar en el extranjero es atractiva. | The idea of studying abroad is appealing.
La ciudad es atractiva por su cultura. | The city is attractive for its culture.
Los nuevos colores del celular son más atractivos. | The new phone colors are more attractive.
Estos precios son bastante atractivos para comprar. | These prices are quite appealing for buying.
Las imágenes en el folleto son muy atractivas. | The images in the brochure are very appealing.
Las playas de México son atractivas para los turistas. | Mexico's beaches are attractive to tourists.

129 – delicioso | **delicious**

El plato que preparó el chef está delicioso. | The dish that the chef prepared is delicious.
Qué aroma delicioso tiene este café recién hecho. | What a delicious aroma this fresh coffee has.
El pastel de chocolate que hiciste está delicioso. | The chocolate cake you made is delicious.
La cena de anoche estuvo deliciosa. | Last night's dinner was delicious.
La sopa de lentejas quedó deliciosa. | The lentil soup turned out delicious.
Tu abuela hace una salsa verde deliciosa. | Your grandma makes a delicious green sauce.
Estos mangos están maduros y deliciosos. | These mangoes are ripe and delicious.
Compramos quesos deliciosos en el mercado. | We bought delicious cheeses at the market.
Las arepas de tu mamá siempre quedan deliciosas. | Your mom's arepas always turn out delicious.
Las papas al horno estaban deliciosas. | The baked potatoes were delicious.

130 – genial | **great, brilliant, awesome**

El profesor nuevo es genial, explica bien. | The new teacher is great, he explains well.
El concierto estuvo genial. | The concert was awesome.
Ese plan suena genial. | That plan sounds great.
La película estuvo genial, me encantó. | The movie was awesome, I loved it.
La fiesta estuvo genial, bailamos toda la noche. | The party was great, we danced all night.
Tu hermana es genial para dar consejos. | Your sister is great at giving advice.
Los amigos de mi hijo son geniales. | My son's friends are great.
Estos libros son geniales, no puedo parar de leer. | These books are awesome, I can't stop reading.
Las canciones de este álbum son geniales. | The songs on this album are brilliant.
Tus ideas para decorar son geniales. | Your decorating ideas are brilliant.

131 – exacto | **exact**

Dame el número exacto de personas que van. | Give me the exact number of people that are going.
No recuerdo el número exacto de invitados. | I don't remember the exact number of guests.
Necesito el dato exacto para el reporte. | I need the exact information for the report.
¿Cuál es la cantidad exacta que debo? | What's the exact amount I owe?
No sé la fecha exacta de su boda. | I don't know the exact date of their wedding.
Necesito la ubicación exacta del hotel. | I need the exact location of the hotel.
Los pasos exactos están escritos en el manual. | The exact steps are written in the manual.
Los detalles exactos los sabremos mañana. | We'll know the exact details tomorrow.
No recuerdo las palabras exactas que dijo. | I don't remember the exact words he said.
Las cifras exactas aparecen en el informe. | The exact figures appear in the report.

132 – perdido | **lost**

Estoy perdido. | I'm lost.
Mi celular está perdido, no lo encuentro. | My phone is lost, I can't find it.
Me siento perdido en esta nueva ciudad. | I feel lost in this new city.
La maleta está perdida desde ayer. | The suitcase has been lost since yesterday.
Mi cartera está perdida. | My wallet is lost.
Se ve perdida con tantas materias nuevas. | She looks lost with so many new subjects.
Los turistas están perdidos. | The tourists are lost.
¿Sabes dónde estamos, o estamos perdidos? | Do you know where we are, or are we lost?
Nuestras maletas siguen perdidas. | Our suitcases are still lost.
Mis llaves están perdidas. | My keys are lost.

133 – oscuro

No me gusta pasar por ese callejón oscuro.
El túnel está muy oscuro y aterrador.
El cielo se pone oscuro antes de la tormenta.
Mi hermano prefiere la ropa oscura.
Esa etapa oscura de mi vida ya terminó.
La casa oscura parece abandonada.
Los jeans oscuros combinan con todo.
Estos días oscuros de invierno me deprimen.
Las calles oscuras no son seguras de noche.
Las nubes oscuras anuncian lluvia.

dark

I don't like walking past that dark alley.
The tunnel is very dark and scary.
The sky gets dark before the storm.
My brother prefers dark clothing.
That dark period of my life is over now.
The dark house looks abandoned.
Dark jeans go with everything.
These dark winter days depress me.
Dark streets aren't safe at night.
Dark clouds announce rain.

134 – molesto

Ese ruido es muy molesto.
Estoy molesto contigo por lo que hiciste.
Mi hermano está molesto porque perdió.
Mi novia está molesta conmigo otra vez.
Esta gripe molesta no se me quita.
Ya llevo una semana con esta tos molesta.
Mis padres están molestos por mis calificaciones.
Los clientes están molestos por la demora.
Las moscas en la cocina son muy molestas.
Mis tías están molestas porque llegamos tarde.

annoying, upset, bothered

That noise is really annoying.
I'm upset with you because of what you did.
My brother is upset because he lost.
My girlfriend is upset with me again.
This annoying flu won't go away.
I've already had this annoying cough for a week.
My parents are upset about my grades.
The customers are upset about the delay.
The flies in the kitchen are very annoying.
My aunts are upset because we arrived late.

135 – humano

El cuerpo humano es increíblemente complejo.
Un error humano causó el accidente.
Errar es humano.
La naturaleza humana no cambia.
La necesidad humana de tener compañía es fuerte.
La fragilidad humana nos recuerda ser humildes.
Los derechos humanos son fundamentales.
Los seres humanos necesitamos dormir mucho.
Las emociones humanas son universales.
Las decisiones humanas no siempre son racionales.

human

The human body is incredibly complex.
Human error caused the accident.
To err is human.
Human nature doesn't change.
The human need to have company is strong.
Human fragility reminds us to be humble.
Human rights are fundamental.
Human beings need to sleep a lot.
Human emotions are universal.
Human decisions are not always rational.

136 – elegante | **elegant, stylish**

Ese reloj es sencillo pero elegante. | That watch is simple but elegant.
El hotel era elegante y cómodo. | The hotel was elegant and comfortable.
Mi papá se ve elegante en ese traje. | My dad looks stylish in that suit.
La decoración es moderna y elegante. | The décor is modern and elegant.
Esa blusa te queda elegante. | That blouse looks elegant on you.
Qué blusa tan elegante, ¿dónde la compraste? | What a stylish blouse, where did you buy it?
Me gustaron los diseños elegantes. | I liked the elegant designs.
Esos zapatos negros son elegantes y cómodos. | Those black shoes are stylish and comfortable.
Mi abuela tiene joyas elegantes. | My grandmother has elegant jewelry.
Venden carteras elegantes pero caras. | They sell elegant but expensive purses.

137 – preocupado | **worried**

El doctor parecía preocupado. | The doctor looked worried.
¿Por qué estás tan preocupado? | Why are you so worried?
Estoy preocupado por mi hijo. | I'm worried about my son.
Ella se veía preocupada en la reunión. | She looked worried in the meeting.
¿Te ves preocupada, qué pasó? | You look worried, what happened?
La vecina está preocupada por su perro enfermo. | The neighbor is worried about her sick dog.
Todos estamos preocupados por el examen final. | We're all worried about the final exam.
Mis papás están preocupados por mí. | My parents are worried about me.
Las mamás estaban preocupadas por sus hijos. | The moms were worried about their kids.
Las enfermeras están preocupadas por los pacientes. | The nurses are worried about the patients.

138 – amplio | **spacious, extensive, broad**

El vestíbulo del hotel es bastante amplio. | The hotel lobby is quite spacious.
Tienen un patio amplio para que los niños jueguen. | They have a spacious yard for the kids to play.
Mi papá tiene un conocimiento amplio sobre carros. | My dad has extensive knowledge about cars.
El apartamento es amplio y luminoso. | The apartment is spacious and bright.
La cocina amplia es ideal para cocinar en familia. | The spacious kitchen is ideal for cooking with family.
Tenemos una amplia experiencia en ventas. | We have extensive experience in sales.
La empresa ofrece una amplia gama de productos. | The company offers a wide range of products.
Los sillones son amplios y perfectos para descansar. | The armchairs are wide and perfect for relaxing.
Tienen amplios conocimientos en tecnología. | They have broad knowledge in technology.
Las calles amplias son más seguras para manejar. | Broad streets are safer for driving.

139 – grave | **serious, severe, deep**

Su estado de salud es grave. | His health condition is serious.
El problema es muy grave para ignorarlo. | The problem is too serious to ignore it.
Mi papá tiene una voz grave. | My dad has a deep voice.
Él tiene una enfermedad grave. | He has a serious illness.
La sequía es muy grave este año. | The drought is very severe this year.
Ella cometió un delito grave. | She committed a serious crime.
Los problemas son muy graves. | The problems are very serious.
Cometieron errores graves. | They made serious mistakes.
Las heridas no son graves. | The wounds are not serious.
Las consecuencias son graves. | The consequences are serious.

140 – dispuesto | **willing, ready, prepared**

Estoy dispuesto a ayudarte en lo que necesites. | I'm willing to help you with whatever you need.
Mi papá no está dispuesto a vender la casa. | My dad isn't willing to sell the house.
Él está dispuesto a trabajar horas extras. | He's willing to work overtime.
Ella está dispuesta a mudarse a otra ciudad. | She's willing to move to another city.
Mi mamá está dispuesta a cuidar a los niños. | My mom is willing to take care of the kids.
Mi hermana está dispuesta a todo por sus niños. | My sister is willing to do anything for her kids.
Los vecinos están dispuestos a limpiar el parque. | The neighbors are willing to clean the park.
Mis hijos están dispuestos a ayudar en casa. | My children are willing to help at home.
Mis tías están dispuestas a organizar la fiesta. | My aunts are willing to organize the party.
Las chicas están dispuestas a quedarse hasta tarde. | The girls are willing to stay late.

141 – firme | **firm, steady, solid**

Él me dio un apretón de manos firme. | He gave me a firm handshake.
Mantén el pie firme en el pedal. | Keep your foot steady on the pedal.
¿El piso es lo suficientemente firme para poner el piano? | Is the floor solid enough to put the piano on it?
Su decisión es firme y no va a cambiar. | Her decision is firm and won't change.
Ella tiene una voz firme cuando habla. | She has a steady voice when she speaks.
La mesa está firme ahora que la arreglamos. | The table is steady now that we fixed it.
Los muros siguen firmes después del temblor. | The walls remain firm after the earthquake.
Ellos permanecieron firmes en su decisión. | They remained firm in their decision.
Los amigos se mantuvieron firmes en su apoyo. | The friends remained firm in their support.
Sus convicciones son firmes. | Her convictions are strong.

142 – privado

Mis hijos van a un colegio privado.
La cantante llegó en un avión privado.
Ese club privado cuesta una fortuna.
Mi esposa tiene una oficina privada.
La universidad privada es demasiado cara.
Mi vida privada no te incumbe.
¿Leíste mis mensajes privados?
Los cursos privados de español son bastante caros.
Las clases privadas ayudan mucho.
Esas áreas privadas no son accesibles.

private

My kids go to a private school.
The singer arrived on a private plane.
That private club costs a fortune.
My wife has a private office.
Private university is too expensive.
My private life doesn't concern you.
Did you read my private messages?
Private Spanish courses are quite expensive.
Private lessons help a lot.
Those private areas are not accessible.

143 – generoso

Él siempre ha sido generoso con los vecinos.
Mi jefe fue generoso con el bono navideño.
Es un hombre generoso de corazón.
La profesora fue generosa al dar más tiempo.
Mi suegra es generosa con los regalos.
Tu mamá fue generosa al prestarnos el carro.
Los voluntarios fueron generosos con su esfuerzo.
Ellos son generosos y siempre comparten.
Las porciones están muy generosas hoy.
Las cantidades son muy generosas en este plato.

generous

He has always been generous with the neighbors.
My boss was generous with the Christmas bonus.
He's a generous man at heart.
The teacher was generous in giving more time.
My mother-in-law is generous with gifts.
Your mom was generous to lend us the car.
The volunteers were generous with their effort.
They are generous and always share.
The portions are very generous today.
The quantities are very generous on this plate.

144 – ancho

El sofá es muy ancho, casi no cabe por la puerta.
Ese río es más ancho de lo que pensaba.
Este pantalón me queda ancho de la cintura.
La mesa es ancha pero no muy larga.
Él tiene la espalda ancha por la natación.
La puerta es ancha para la silla de ruedas.
Mi primo tiene los hombros muy anchos.
Me gusta usar cinturones anchos con los jeans.
Las escaleras anchas facilitan el paso de personas.
Las alas del avión son muy anchas.

wide

The sofa is really wide, it barely fits through the door.
That river is wider than I thought.
These pants are too wide at the waist.
The table is wide but not very long.
He has a broad back from swimming.
The door is wide for the wheelchair.
My cousin has very broad shoulders.
I like to wear wide belts with jeans.
The wide stairs make it easier for people to pass.
The airplane wings are very wide.

145 – curioso — **curious, odd**

El niño curioso abrió todos los cajones. — The curious boy opened all the drawers.
Fue curioso lo que dijo el profesor hoy. — It was odd what the professor said today.
Siempre he sido curioso con los temas de ciencia. — I've always been curious about science topics.
Mi hermana es muy curiosa. — My sister is really nosy.
Él tiene una forma curiosa de ver la vida. — He has a curious way of seeing life.
Me parece curiosa la forma en la que él habla. — I find the way he speaks curious.
Los gatos son animales muy curiosos. — Cats are very curious animals.
Los niños son curiosos por naturaleza. — Kids are naturally curious.
Esas coincidencias son muy curiosas. — Those coincidences are quite odd.
Mis hijas son muy curiosas con los insectos. — My daughters are very curious about insects.

146 – adecuado — **suitable, appropriate, right**

No es el momento adecuado para hablar de esto. — It's not the right moment to talk about this.
No es un lugar adecuado para niños. — It's not a suitable place for kids.
El clima no es adecuado para hacer una parrillada. — The weather isn't suitable for having a barbecue.
La música no era adecuada para el restaurante. — The music was not suitable for the restaurant.
Estoy buscando una escuela adecuada para mi hija. — I'm looking for a suitable school for my daughter.
La ropa adecuada depende del evento. — The appropriate clothing depends on the event.
Esos zapatos no son adecuados para correr. — Those shoes aren't suitable for running.
Tus comentarios no fueron adecuados. — Your comments weren't appropriate.
Sus palabras fueron muy adecuadas para la ocasión. — Her words were very appropriate for the occasion.
Las herramientas adecuadas facilitan el trabajo. — The right tools make the job easier.

147 – alegre — **happy, cheerful**

Me gusta trabajar con alguien tan alegre como tú. — I like working with someone as cheerful as you.
Juan siempre ha sido un tipo alegre y divertido. — Juan has always been a cheerful and fun guy.
El profesor vino más alegre de lo normal hoy. — The teacher came in happier than usual today.
Mi hermana es alegre y siempre sonríe. — My sister is cheerful and always smiles.
Mi abuela siempre fue una mujer muy alegre. — My grandmother was always a cheerful woman.
Es una canción muy alegre. — It's a very upbeat song.
Los invitados estaban alegres y bailando. — The guests were cheerful and dancing.
Me encantan los colores alegres para decorar la casa. — I love cheerful colors for decorating the house.
Las canciones alegres son perfectas para bailar. — Upbeat songs are perfect for dancing.
Las voces alegres de los niños llenaban el parque. — The cheerful voices of the children filled the park.

148 – emocionado | **excited**

Estoy emocionado por el viaje a México. — I'm excited about the trip to Mexico.
El niño está emocionado por su cumpleaños. — The boy is excited about his birthday.
Mi papá está emocionado por su primer nieto. — My dad is excited about his first grandchild.
Mi mamá está emocionada por su nuevo trabajo. — My mom is excited about her new job.
Estaba emocionada por escuchar su canción favorita. — She was excited to hear her favorite song.
Ana está emocionada por la graduación. — Ana is excited about graduation.
Los niños están emocionados por las vacaciones. — The kids are excited about vacation.
Mis papás están emocionados por el bebé. — My parents are excited about the baby.
Ellas están emocionadas por la fiesta. — They're excited about the party.
Estamos emocionadas por el reencuentro. — We're excited about the reunion.

149 – fantástico | **fantastic**

El concierto estuvo fantástico. — The concert was fantastic.
Mi vecino de al lado es fantástico. — My next-door neighbor is fantastic.
Qué día tan fantástico para ir a la playa. — What a fantastic day to go to the beach.
La vista desde aquí es fantástica. — The view from here is fantastic.
Esa idea para el proyecto estuvo fantástica. — That idea for the project was fantastic.
La comida de este restaurante es fantástica. — The food at this restaurant is fantastic.
Tus hijos son futbolistas fantásticos. — Your boys are fantastic soccer players.
Los precios en esa tienda son fantásticos. — The prices at that store are fantastic.
Mis abuelos son personas fantásticas. — My grandparents are fantastic people.
Tengo noticias fantásticas. — I have fantastic news.

150 – mojado | **wet**

El piso está mojado, ten cuidado. — The floor is wet, be careful.
No te sientes en ese asiento, está mojado. — Don't sit in that seat, it's wet.
El perro entró todo mojado a la sala. — The dog came into the living room all wet.
La tierra está mojada por la lluvia. — The ground is wet from the rain.
¿Por qué dejaste la toalla mojada en la cama? — Why did you leave the wet towel on the bed?
Una camiseta mojada se pega a la piel. — A wet t-shirt sticks to your skin.
Mis zapatos están mojados por el charco. — My shoes are wet from the puddle.
Dejaron los paraguas mojados en la entrada. — They left the wet umbrellas at the entrance.
Estas toallas todavía están mojadas. — These towels are still wet.
Las escaleras mojadas son peligrosas. — Wet stairs are dangerous.

151 – breve | **brief**

El mensaje fue breve y claro. | The message was brief and clear.
Su discurso fue breve pero emotivo. | His speech was brief but moving.
¿Puedes hacer un resumen breve de lo que pasó? | Can you give a brief summary of what happened?
Fue una visita muy breve. | It was a very brief visit.
Hubo una pausa breve en la conversación. | There was a brief pause in the conversation.
Tuvimos una conversación breve en el pasillo. | We had a brief conversation in the hallway.
Sus comentarios fueron breves pero certeros. | His comments were brief but accurate.
Los capítulos de este libro son breves y fáciles de leer. | The chapters in this book are brief and easy to read.
Tuvimos conversaciones breves con cada candidato. | We had brief conversations with each candidate.
Las instrucciones breves son más fáciles de seguir. | Brief instructions are easier to follow.

152 – enojado | **angry**

Estoy enojado contigo por no decirme la verdad. | I'm mad at you for not telling me the truth.
Mi papá está enojado por alguna razón. | My dad is angry for some reason.
Está tan enojado que ni me quiere hablar. | He's so mad he doesn't even want to talk to me.
No entiendo por qué estás tan enojada conmigo. | I don't understand why you're so mad at me.
Mamá estaba enojada, pero ya se le pasó. | Mom was angry, but she's over it now.
Está enojada porque le cancelaron el vuelo. | She's angry because they canceled her flight.
Los vecinos están enojados por el ruido. | The neighbors are angry about the noise.
Los niños están enojados por el viaje cancelado. | The kids are mad about the canceled trip.
Mis amigas están enojadas porque les mentí. | My friends are angry because I lied to them.
Tenían razón de estar enojadas. | They were right to be angry.

153 – profundo | **deep**

¿Qué tan profundo es el río en esa parte? | How deep is the river in that part?
Él tiene un conocimiento profundo del tema. | He has a deep knowledge of the subject.
Es un tema profundo que requiere mucho estudio. | It's a profound topic that requires a lot of study.
La piscina es profunda en este lado. | The pool is deep on this side.
Tengo una herida profunda en la pierna. | I have a deep wound on my leg.
Sentí una tristeza profunda cuando murió mi madre. | I felt a deep sadness when my mother died.
Tienen sentimientos profundos el uno por el otro. | They have deep feelings for each other.
Los buzos exploraron los océanos profundos. | The divers explored the deep oceans.
Le ofrecieron disculpas profundas por el error. | They offered her deep apologies for the mistake.
Mis abuelas tienen profundas creencias religiosas. | My grandmothers have deep religious beliefs.

154 – efectivo | **effective**

Este jarabe es efectivo para la tos.	This syrup is effective for coughs.
Es un método muy efectivo.	It's a very effective method.
Ese remedio es efectivo contra la gripe.	That remedy is effective against the flu.
Esa crema es efectiva para las quemaduras leves.	That cream is effective for mild burns.
Encontramos una solución efectiva al problema.	We found an effective solution to the problem.
La campaña en redes sociales fue efectiva.	The campaign on social media was effective.
Los ejercicios del fisioterapeuta fueron efectivos.	The physical therapist's exercises were effective.
Estos productos son efectivos contra las manchas.	These products are effective against stains.
Estas pastillas son efectivas para dormir mejor.	These pills are effective for sleeping better.
Las campañas de vacunación fueron efectivas.	The vaccination campaigns were effective.

155 – gracioso | **funny**

Mi papá se ve gracioso con bigote.	My dad looks funny with a mustache.
Eso no fue gracioso, fue molesto.	That wasn’t funny, it was annoying.
Es el chiste más gracioso que he oído.	That's the funniest joke I've ever heard.
Esa película es muy graciosa, tienes que verla.	That movie is really funny, you have to watch it.
Tu hermana se cree graciosa, pero no lo es.	Your sister thinks she's funny, but she's not.
Qué graciosa manera de decirlo.	What a funny way to say it.
Los payasos de circo no son graciosos.	Circus clowns are not funny.
Los perros son graciosos cuando persiguen su cola.	Dogs are funny when they chase their tail.
Mi abuelo cuenta historias graciosas.	My grandpa tells funny stories.
Esa película tiene partes graciosas.	That movie has funny parts.

156 – roto | **broken**

Ya no sirve, está roto.	It doesn't work anymore, it's broken.
Ella tiene el corazón roto.	She has a broken heart.
¿Cómo enciendo la tele si el control está roto?	How do I turn on the tv if the remote is broken?
La lavadora está rota.	The washing machine is broken.
La pantalla de mi celular está rota.	The screen on my cellphone is broken.
Hay una ventana rota en el segundo piso.	There's a broken window on the second floor.
Los vasos que estaban en el lavaplatos están rotos.	The glasses that were in the dishwasher are broken.
¡Ay, no, mis audífonos están rotos!	Oh no, my headphones are broken!
Las botellas llegaron rotas del envío.	The bottles arrived broken from the shipment.
Las cortinas están rotas y no bajan.	The blinds are broken and won’t go down.

157 – activo	**active**
Mi abuelo sigue activo a los ochenta años.	My grandfather is still active at eighty years old.
Mi perro es muy activo y necesita cinco paseos al día.	My dog is really active and needs five walks per day.
El volcán está activo desde hace tres meses.	The volcano has been active for three months.
Tengo una vida social activa los fines de semana.	I have an active social life on weekends.
Ella se mantiene activa caminando todos los días.	She stays active by walking every day.
Mi abuela es muy activa para su edad.	My grandma is very active for her age.
Mis hijos son muy activos en deportes.	My kids are very active in sports.
Los bomberos permanecen activos toda la noche.	The firefighters remain active all night.
Las abejas son más activas en el verano.	Bees are more active in the summer.
Ellas son activas en causas sociales.	They are active in social causes.

158 – entretenido	**entertaining**
El recorrido por el museo estuvo entretenido.	The tour through the museum was entertaining.
El libro que me prestaste es muy entretenido.	The book you lent me is very entertaining.
Carlos siempre hace entretenido cualquier viaje.	Carlos always makes any trip entertaining.
La película estuvo entretenida.	The movie was entertaining.
Es entretenido hablar con mi tía.	It's entertaining to talk to my aunt.
La obra de teatro me pareció entretenida.	I found the play entertaining.
Los cuentos de la maestra fueron entretenidos.	The teacher's stories were entertaining.
Los niños están entretenidos con los juguetes.	The kids are entertained with the toys.
Estas series coreanas son entretenidas.	These Korean series are entertaining.
Las niñas están entretenidas haciendo pulseras.	The girls are entertained making bracelets.

159 – maravilloso	**wonderful, marvelous, amazing**
Tuvimos un viaje maravilloso.	We had a wonderful trip.
Me parece maravilloso que vengas.	I think it's wonderful that you're coming.
Tu hijo es un niño maravilloso y se comporta bien.	Your son is a wonderful child and behaves well.
Tienes una voz maravillosa.	You have an amazing voice.
Fue una experiencia maravillosa.	It was a wonderful experience.
Qué idea tan maravillosa.	What a wonderful idea.
Los postres de la fiesta estaban maravillosos.	The desserts at the party were wonderful.
Tenemos amigos maravillosos que siempre ayudan.	We have wonderful friends who always help.
Las flores de tu jardín están maravillosas este año.	The flowers in your garden are amazing this year.
Tus hermanas son maravillosas, me caen muy bien.	Your sisters are wonderful, I like them very much.

160 – enamorado | **in love**

Estoy enamorado de ella. | I'm in love with her.
Nunca lo había visto tan enamorado. | I had never seen him so in love.
Nunca he estado tan enamorado en mi vida. | I have never been this in love in my life.
Estoy completamente enamorada de mi novio. | I'm completely in love with my boyfriend.
Se ve enamorada, ¿no crees? | She looks like she's in love, don't you think?
La vecina está enamorada de un hombre casado. | The neighbor is in love with a married man.
Todos mis amigos están enamorados menos yo. | All my friends are in love except me.
Parecían dos adolescentes enamorados. | They looked like two teenagers in love.
Las gemelas están enamoradas del mismo chico. | The twins are in love with the same guy.
No paran de hablar, están enamoradas. | They won't stop talking, they're in love.

161 – sano | **healthy**

No hay nada más valioso que estar sano. | Nothing is more valuable than being healthy.
El bebé nació sano. | The baby was born healthy.
Quiero comer algo sano. | I want to eat something healthy.
La comida rápida no es muy sana. | Fast food isn't very healthy.
Dormir bien es parte de una vida sana. | Sleeping well is part of a healthy life.
Ella lleva una vida sana. | She leads a healthy life.
Mis hijos están bastante sanos. | My kids are quite healthy.
Tus nietos se ven sanos. | Your grandkids look healthy.
¿Tienen opciones sanas en este restaurante? | Do you have healthy options at this restaurant?
Las costumbres sanas se aprenden de niños. | Healthy habits are learned as kids.

162 – educado | **polite, well-mannered, well-behaved**

Si eres educado, la gente te trata mejor. | If you're polite, people treat you better.
Mi hijo es muy educado con los mayores. | My son is very polite with older people.
Ese niño es muy educado. | That boy is very well-behaved.
Mi vecina siempre ha sido muy educada. | My neighbor has always been very polite.
Ella siempre es educada. | She's always polite.
Su hija es educada, siempre da las gracias. | Her daughter is polite, she always says thanks.
Mis hijos no son educados. | My children are not well-mannered.
Los hijos de Marta son súper educados. | Marta's kids are super well-mannered.
Las profesoras eran educadas pero estrictas. | The teachers were polite but strict.
Prefiero tratar con personas educadas. | I prefer dealing with polite people.

163 – asustado | **scared, frightened, startled**

El niño está asustado por la tormenta. | The boy is scared because of the storm.
Juan salió asustado de la película de terror. | Juan came out scared from the horror movie.
Él estaba tan asustado que no podía ni hablar. | He was so scared he couldn't even speak.
La niñita perdida estaba asustada. | The lost little girl was scared.
Mi hermana se veía asustada durante la tormenta. | My sister looked scared during the storm.
Ana se sintió asustada caminando sola de noche. | Ana felt scared walking alone at night.
Los niños están asustados por los truenos. | The children are scared of the thunder.
Los pasajeros estaban asustados durante la turbulencia. | The passengers were scared during the turbulence.
Las niñas están asustadas por el perro del vecino. | The girls are scared of the neighbor's dog.
Las mamás están asustadas por lo que pasó en el colegio. | The moms are scared about what happened at school.

164 – cariñoso | **loving, affectionate**

Tu novio parece muy cariñoso contigo. | Your boyfriend seems very loving with you.
Me encanta lo cariñoso que es tu abuelo. | I love how affectionate your grandpa is.
Mi hijo es muy cariñoso conmigo. | My son is very affectionate with me.
Mi mamá siempre fue muy cariñosa. | My mom was always very affectionate.
Tu hija está muy cariñosa contigo hoy. | Your daughter is very affectionate with you today.
Mi suegra es bastante cariñosa, por suerte. | My mother-in-law is quite loving, fortunately.
Son niños cariñosos. | They're affectionate kids.
Estos gatitos son cariñosos con todo el mundo. | These kittens are loving with everyone.
Mis hermanas son cariñosas entre ellas. | My sisters are affectionate with each other.
Las abuelas son cariñosas con sus nietos. | Grandmothers are loving with their grandchildren.

165 – suave | **smooth, soft**

Me gusta mucho tu suéter suave. | I really like your soft sweater.
Tuvimos un aterrizaje suave en Cancún. | We had a smooth landing in Cancún.
Tu perro tiene el pelaje muy suave. | Your dog has very soft fur.
La piel del bebé es muy suave. | The baby's skin is so soft.
Prefiero la música suave. | I prefer soft music.
La seda se siente suave. | Silk feels soft.
Prefiero los quesos suaves a los fuertes. | I prefer mild cheeses to strong ones.
Los movimientos suaves relajan el cuerpo. | Gentle movements relax the body.
Las voces suaves me relajan mucho. | Soft voices relax me a lot.
Las luces suaves crean un ambiente acogedor. | Soft lighting creates a cozy atmosphere.

166 – ruidoso

Tu perro es ruidoso cuando duerme.
Está muy ruidoso aquí, no se puede hablar.
El bar de la esquina siempre es ruidoso.
Vivo en una calle ruidosa.
La fiesta fue ruidosa, pero divertida.
La calle está ruidosa por el tráfico.
No me gustan los lugares ruidosos.
No puedo creer lo ruidosos que son nuestros vecinos.
Las chicas ruidosas no dejan de chillar.
Mi esposa y yo venimos de familias ruidosas.

noisy

Your dog is noisy when he sleeps.
It's very noisy here, you can't talk.
The bar on the corner is always noisy.
I live on a noisy street.
The party was noisy but fun.
The street is noisy because of traffic.
I don't like noisy places.
I can't believe how noisy our neighbors are.
The noisy girls won't stop shrieking.
My wife and I come from noisy families.

167 – picante

Está muy picante, no puedo comerlo.
¿Quieres algo menos picante?
¿Tienen algún plato que no sea picante?
Me encantan los tacos con salsa picante.
No me gusta la comida picante.
La salsa está picante, ten cuidado.
Las papas fritas picantes estaban deliciosas.
Las alitas picantes son muy populares.
Estas alitas están picantes.
Las salsas mexicanas son muy picantes.

spicy

It's too spicy, I can't eat it.
Do you want something less spicy?
Do you have any dish that isn't spicy?
I love tacos with spicy sauce.
I don't like spicy food.
The sauce is spicy, be careful.
The spicy fries were delicious.
Spicy wings are very popular.
These wings are spicy.
Mexican sauces are very spicy.

168 – independiente

Él quiere ser independiente y mudarse pronto.
Me siento independiente cuando gano mi propio dinero.
El productor independiente financió toda la película.
La señora es independiente y todavía vive sola.
Prefiero una vida independiente a depender de otros.
La tienda independiente cerró por la competencia.
Mis hijos ya son independientes y viven solos.
Los niños independientes hacen su tarea solos.
Las peluquerías independientes tienen clientela fiel.
Ellas son independientes y no dependen de nadie.

independent

He wants to be independent and move out soon.
I feel independent when I earn my own money.
The independent producer financed the entire movie.
The lady is independent and still lives alone.
I prefer an independent life to depending on others.
The independent store closed due to competition.
My children are already independent and live alone.
Independent kids do their homework alone.
Independent hair salons have loyal clientele.
They are independent and don't depend on anyone.

169 – blando | **soft**

Este plátano está muy blando, lo usaré para hacer pan. | This banana is very soft, I'll use it to make bread.
Este colchón es demasiado blando para mi espalda. | This mattress is too soft for my back.
No seas tan blando con los empleados que llegan tarde. | Don't be so soft on late employees.
Me gusta la mantequilla blanda que se unta fácilmente. | I like soft butter that's easy to spread.
Esta silla está muy blanda, me hundo del todo. | This chair is very soft, I sink completely into it.
La tierra está blanda por la lluvia de anoche. | The ground is soft from last night's rain.
Me gustan los caramelos blandos, no los duros. | I like soft candies, not the hard ones.
Los niños de hoy son blandos. | Kids today are soft.
Las frutas ya están blandas, hay que comérselas hoy. | The fruits are already soft, we have to eat them today.
Mi hijo prefiere verduras blandas. | My son prefers soft vegetables.

170 – romántico | **romantic**

Regalar flores es un detalle romántico. | It's a romantic gesture to give flowers.
El ambiente del restaurante es romántico. | The restaurant's atmosphere is romantic.
Lo admito, no soy nada romántico. | I admit it, I'm not romantic at all.
Él me escribió una carta romántica. | He wrote me a romantic letter.
Hicimos una escapada romántica al campo. | We took a romantic getaway to the countryside.
París es una ciudad romántica. | Paris is a romantic city.
La ciudad tiene muchos lugares románticos. | The city has many romantic spots.
Los gestos románticos ya no se ven mucho. | Romantic gestures aren't seen much anymore.
Las comedias románticas son mis películas favoritas. | Romantic comedies are my favorite movies.
Me encantan las historias románticas con final feliz. | I love romantic stories with a happy ending.

171 – callado | **quiet, reserved**

Mi hermano es callado en las reuniones familiares. | My brother is quiet at family gatherings.
Mi papá es callado por naturaleza. | My dad is quiet by nature.
Juan parece callado, pero piensa mucho. | Juan seems quiet, but he thinks a lot.
Mi mamá estuvo callada toda la cena. | My mom was quiet the whole dinner.
La niña callada de al lado siempre está leyendo. | The quiet girl next door is always reading.
María es callada pero muy trabajadora. | María is quiet but very hardworking.
Necesitamos estar callados en la biblioteca. | We need to be quiet in the library.
Nos quedamos callados para no interrumpir. | We stayed quiet so we wouldn't interrupt.
Las nuevas compañeras son un poco calladas. | The new classmates are a bit quiet.
Mis hermanas son calladas cuando hay visitas. | My sisters are quiet when there are visitors.

172 – puro

pure

Este café es sabor colombiano puro. — This coffee is pure Colombian flavor.
El anillo es de oro puro. — The ring is made of pure gold.
El aire puro de la montaña es refrescante. — The pure mountain air is refreshing.
La plata pura es más blanda que el oro puro. — Pure silver is softer than pure gold.
Los gatos de raza pura son difíciles de encontrar. — Purebred cats are hard to find.
En Costa Rica dicen mucho "pura vida". — In Costa Rica they say "pura vida" (pure life) a lot.
Estos ingredientes son puros y naturales. — These ingredients are pure and natural.
Los extractos puros de hierbas son más efectivos. — Pure herbal extracts are more effective.
Son puras excusas para no ir. — They're pure excuses for not going.
Quiero vitaminas puras sin relleno. — I want pure vitamins without filler.

173 – tradicional

traditional

Este es un baile tradicional de mi país. — This is a traditional dance from my country.
El mole es un platillo tradicional de México. — Mole is a traditional dish from Mexico.
Mi abuelo es muy tradicional en sus costumbres. — My grandfather is very traditional in his customs.
La feria tiene una decoración tradicional colorida. — The fair has colorful traditional decoration.
Prefiero una boda tradicional a una moderna. — I prefer a traditional wedding to a modern one.
Mi familia es muy tradicional y religiosa. — My family is very traditional and religious.
Me gustan los postres tradicionales de Navidad. — I like traditional Christmas desserts.
Vendemos productos tradicionales hechos a mano. — We sell traditional handmade products.
Mis tías cocinan sopas tradicionales muy sabrosas. — My aunts cook very tasty traditional soups.
Las costumbres tradicionales siguen vivas en el pueblo. — Traditional customs remain alive in the town.

174 – nervioso

nervous

Estoy nervioso por la entrevista de mañana. — I'm nervous about tomorrow's interview.
Él se puso nervioso cuando lo llamaron al frente. — He got nervous when they called him to the front.
Siempre me pongo nervioso en las citas. — I always get nervous on dates.
Mi hermana está nerviosa por su boda. — My sister is nervous about her wedding.
Ella se veía nerviosa en la reunión. — She looked nervous in the meeting.
La profesora estaba nerviosa el primer día. — The teacher was nervous on the first day.
Los jugadores se pusieron nerviosos en la final. — The players got nervous in the final.
Los estudiantes estaban nerviosos antes del examen. — The students were nervous before the test.
Las profesoras están nerviosas por el nuevo director. — The teachers are nervous about the new principal.
Las niñas se pusieron nerviosas en la competencia. — The girls got nervous at the competition.

175 – poderoso — **powerful, strong**

Es un empresario poderoso con mucha influencia.	He's a powerful businessman with a lot of influence.
Él tiene un mensaje poderoso que inspira a todos.	He has a powerful message that inspires everyone.
Mi abuelo era un hombre poderoso en los negocios.	My grandfather was a powerful man in business.
El presidente es una persona poderosa.	The president is a powerful person.
Su voz es poderosa cuando canta ópera.	Her voice is powerful when she sings opera.
La naturaleza es poderosa y a veces destructiva.	Nature is powerful and sometimes destructive.
Los rayos del sol son muy poderosos al mediodía.	The sun's rays are very powerful at noon.
Los vientos eran poderosos durante la tormenta.	The winds were strong during the storm.
Ayer, las olas estaban poderosas en la playa.	Yesterday the waves were powerful at the beach.
Sus palabras fueron poderosas y convincentes.	Her words were powerful and convincing.

176 – creativo — **creative**

Ser creativo te ayuda en cualquier trabajo.	Being creative helps in any job.
Ese niño es creativo con sus dibujos.	That kid is creative with his drawings.
Este artista callejero es increíblemente creativo.	This street artist is incredibly creative.
Esa solución fue muy creativa de tu parte.	That solution was very creative on your part.
Tu hermana tiene una mente muy creativa.	Your sister has a very creative mind.
Esa niña es creativa hasta con los disfraces.	That girl is creative even with costumes.
Los niños son más creativos de lo que tú crees.	Kids are more creative than you think.
Sus anuncios son siempre muy creativos.	Their ads are always very creative.
¿Las niñas son más creativas que los niños?	Are girls more creative than boys?
Las soluciones que propusieron fueron creativas.	The solutions they proposed were quite creative.

177 – estrecho — **narrow**

El callejón es tan estrecho que apenas pasa una bici.	The alley is so narrow that only a bike fits.
El puente estrecho solo permite un carro a la vez.	The narrow bridge only allows one car at a time.
Este pantalón me queda muy estrecho en la cintura.	These pants are too tight at the waist.
La escalera es muy estrecha.	The staircase is really narrow.
La puerta estrecha dificulta meter los muebles.	The narrow door makes it hard to bring in furniture.
Esta blusa me queda estrecha.	This blouse is tight on me.
Estos zapatos me quedaron demasiado estrechos.	These shoes turned out too tight.
Los caminos de montaña son estrechos.	The mountain roads are narrow.
Tenemos lazos muy estrechos.	We have very close ties.
Las calles del centro son estrechas.	The downtown streets are narrow.

178 – maduro | **mature, ripe**

El plátano está maduro. | The banana is ripe.
¿Cómo puedo saber si el aguacate está maduro? | How can I tell if the avocado is ripe?
El queso maduro tiene más sabor. | Mature cheese has more flavor.
Ella es muy madura para su edad. | She's very mature for her age.
Él tomó una decisión madura para ser tan joven. | He made a mature decision for being so young.
Ella es más madura que sus amigas. | She is more mature than her friends.
Los aguacates maduros son suaves y cremosos. | Ripe avocados are soft and creamy.
Gracias por sus comentarios maduros y reflexivos. | Thank you for the mature and thoughtful comments.
Las chicas suelen ser más maduras que los chicos. | Girls tend to be more mature than boys.
Las manzanas están maduras y se caen del árbol. | The apples are ripe and falling off the tree.

179 – brillante | **brilliant, bright, shiny**

El sol está demasiado brillante, no puedo ver. | The sun is too bright, I can't see.
Ese niño es brillante en matemáticas. | That kid is brilliant at math.
El diamante se ve más brillante con esa luz. | The diamond looks brighter under that light.
La luna está brillante esta noche. | The moon is bright tonight.
Ella tiene una mente brillante e ideas geniales. | She has a brilliant mind and has great ideas.
Fue una jugada brillante del delantero. | It was a brilliant play by the forward.
Los resultados brillantes del equipo nos sorprendieron. | The brilliant results of the team surprised us.
Los faros brillantes iluminan bien la carretera. | The bright headlights illuminate the road well.
Tus ideas brillantes ayudaron mucho al equipo. | Your brilliant ideas helped the team a lot.
Las monedas brillantes salieron de la casa de la moneda. | The shiny coins came from the mint.

180 – optimista | **optimistic**

El doctor fue optimista sobre la cirugía. | The doctor was optimistic about the surgery.
Estoy optimista sobre mi entrevista mañana. | I'm optimistic about my interview tomorrow.
Estoy tratando de ser más optimista. | I'm trying to be more optimistic.
Mi mamá es la persona más optimista que conozco. | My mother is the most optimistic person I know.
Mi hermana es optimista con su nuevo negocio. | My sister is optimistic about her new business.
Me gusta la gente optimista. | I like optimistic people.
Los jóvenes son más optimistas sobre el cambio. | Young people are more optimistic about change.
Los inversionistas están optimistas este año. | Investors are optimistic this year.
Las proyecciones económicas son optimistas. | The economic projections are optimistic.
Las empresas están optimistas sobre el mercado. | Companies are optimistic about the market.

181 – inútil

useless

Me siento inútil cuando no puedo ayudar.
Fue inútil intentar convencerla.
Este celular viejo es inútil, ya ni prende.
La información que me diste es inútil.
La reunión de ayer me pareció inútil.
Esa llave doblada es inútil ahora.
Esos consejos inútiles no ayudan en nada.
Los métodos antiguos ya son inútiles.
Tus quejas son inútiles, nada va a cambiar.
Las instrucciones en chino son inútiles para mí.

I feel useless when I can't help.
It was useless trying to convince her.
This old phone is useless, it doesn't even turn on.
The information you gave me is useless.
Yesterday's meeting seemed useless to me.
That bent key is useless now.
Those useless tips don't help at all.
The old methods are already useless.
Your complaints are useless, nothing will change.
The instructions in Chinese are useless to me.

182 – ciego

blind

Mi abuelo está ciego por la diabetes.
Está ciego de amor.
Mi hermano está ciego de ira.
La gata ciega encuentra su comida por el olfato.
Está ciega ante las mentiras de su esposo.
A veces la gente está ciega ante la injusticia.
Muchos ciegos usan bastones para orientarse.
Todos somos ciegos cuando se trata del amor.
Las personas ciegas desarrollan mejor el oído.
Las mujeres ciegas usan tecnología especial.

My grandfather is blind because of diabetes.
He's blinded by love.
My brother is blind with rage.
The blind cat finds her food by smell.
She's blind to her husband's lies.
Sometimes people are blind to injustice.
Many blind people use canes to get around.
We're all blind when it comes to love.
Blind people develop better hearing.
The blind women use special technology.

183 – estúpido

stupid

No seas estúpido, claro que te quiero.
Me siento estúpido por haber creído eso.
Fue estúpido de mi parte decir eso.
Esa regla es completamente estúpida.
Mi jefe tomó una decisión estúpida.
La pregunta me pareció estúpida.
Qué estúpidos fuimos al creerle.
Se ven estúpidos discutiendo por tonterías.
Las peleas por tonterías son estúpidas.
Tomaron decisiones estúpidas por la prisa.

Don't be stupid, of course I love you.
I feel stupid for having believed that.
It was stupid of me to say that.
That rule is completely stupid.
My boss made a stupid decision.
The question seemed stupid to me.
How stupid we were to believe him.
They look stupid arguing over nonsense.
Fights over silly things are stupid.
They made stupid decisions out of haste.

184 – celoso | **jealous**

Mi novio se puso celoso cuando hablé con mi ex. | My boyfriend got jealous when I talked to my ex.
Se pone celoso fácilmente. | He gets jealous easily.
No te pongas celoso, solo es mi amigo. | Don't be jealous, he's just my friend.
Mi perrita se pone celosa cuando acaricio al gato. | My dog gets jealous when I pet the cat.
Está celosa de la casa nueva de su vecina. | She's jealous of her neighbor's new house.
Ana está celosa de su mejor amiga. | Ana is jealous of her best friend.
Mis hijos están celosos del nuevo bebé. | My kids are jealous of the new baby.
Están celosos de su éxito. | They're jealous of his success.
Las estudiantes están celosas de la beca de Sofía. | The students are jealous of Sofía's scholarship.
Eran muy celosas y siempre competían. | They were very jealous and always competing.

185 – emocionante | **exciting, thrilling, moving**

Ese libro tiene un final muy emocionante. | That book has a very exciting ending.
El final de la película fue emocionante. | The end of the movie was exciting.
El partido estuvo emocionante hasta el final. | The game was exciting until the end.
Esa montaña rusa es emocionante. | That roller coaster is exciting.
La película fue tan emocionante que casi lloro. | The movie was so moving that I almost cried.
Su historia de vida es realmente emocionante. | Her life story is really exciting.
Mudarnos a otra ciudad es emocionante. | Moving to another city is exciting.
Los primeros días fueron los más emocionantes. | The first days were the most exciting.
Estas nuevas oportunidades son emocionantes. | These new opportunities are exciting.
Nuestras vacaciones fueron emocionantes. | Our vacation was exciting.

186 – tímido | **shy, timid**

Es tan tímido que nunca levanta la mano en clase. | He's so shy that he never raises his hand in class.
Era tímido de chico pero ya cambió mucho. | He was shy as a kid but he's changed a lot.
El niño tímido no quería saludar. | The shy boy didn't want to say hello.
Mi hija es tímida con extraños. | My daughter is shy with strangers.
La alumna tímida no levantó la mano. | The shy student didn't raise her hand.
La niña tímida se escondió detrás de su mamá. | The shy girl hid behind her mom.
Los niños tímidos miraban el piso en vez de contestar. | The shy kids looked at the floor instead of answering.
Son tímidos con las chicas que les gustan. | They're shy with girls they like.
Las niñas tímidas se escondieron detrás de la cortina. | The shy girls hid behind the curtain.
Mis hijas no suelen ser tan tímidas. | My daughters aren't usually so shy.

187 – fijo | **fixed**

Ya casi nadie usa teléfono fijo. | Almost nobody uses a landline anymore.
Mi horario de trabajo es fijo de lunes a viernes. | My work schedule is fixed from Monday to Friday.
Él me miró con una mirada fija. | He looked at me with a steady gaze.
Tengo una rutina fija todas las mañanas. | I have a fixed routine every morning.
La fecha de la boda ya está fija. | The wedding date is already set.
Ella tiene una idea fija en la cabeza. | She has a fixed idea in her head.
Los horarios son fijos. | The schedules are fixed.
Mis gastos fijos son altos. | My fixed expenses are high.
Las tarifas son fijas, no varían. | The rates are fixed, they don't vary.
Mis clases son a horas fijas. | My classes are at fixed times.

188 – lejano | **distant, far**

Ese recuerdo lejano todavía me hace sonreír. | That distant memory still makes me smile.
Parece un sueño lejano ahora. | It seems like a distant dream now.
Escucho el trueno lejano de una tormenta. | I hear the distant thunder of a storm.
Veo una montaña lejana en el horizonte. | I see a distant mountain on the horizon.
Se escucha música lejana de una fiesta. | You can hear distant music from a party.
En mi lejana infancia todo parecía más sencillo. | In my distant childhood everything seemed simpler.
Tengo algunos parientes lejanos en Canadá. | I have a few distant relatives in Canada.
Estos recuerdos lejanos me dan nostalgia. | These distant memories make me nostalgic.
Desde aquí puedes ver las luces lejanas del puerto. | From here you can see the distant lights of the port.
Siempre soñé con viajar a tierras lejanas. | I always dreamed of traveling to faraway lands.

189 – amigable | **friendly**

Mis compañeros de trabajo son muy amigables. | My coworkers are really friendly.
Mi perro es muy amigable, siempre quiere jugar. | My dog is really friendly, he always wants to play.
Los vecinos fueron amigables cuando nos mudamos. | The neighbors were friendly when we moved in.
La señora de la tienda es súper amigable. | The lady at the store is super friendly.
Ella tiene una sonrisa amigable que inspira confianza. | She has a friendly smile that inspires trust.
Tu mamá siempre ha sido muy amigable conmigo. | Your mom has always been very friendly to me.
Los vendedores son muy amigables en esa tienda. | The salespeople are really friendly in that store.
Me sorprendió lo amigables que fueron todos. | I was surprised by how friendly everyone was.
Tus hermanos parecen muy amigables. | Your siblings seem very friendly.
Hay personas amigables en todas partes. | There are friendly people everywhere.

190 – desnudo | **naked, nude**

El bebé estaba desnudo corriendo por la casa. | The baby was naked running around the house.
El árbol quedó desnudo tras perder sus hojas. | The tree was left bare after losing its leaves.
El modelo posó desnudo para la clase de arte. | The model posed nude for the art class.
La montaña se ve desnuda sin nieve. | The mountain looks bare without snow.
La mujer se sintió desnuda sin su maquillaje. | The woman felt naked without her makeup.
La actriz apareció desnuda en la película. | The actress appeared nude in the movie.
En la playa nudista, todos estaban desnudos. | At the nudist beach, everyone was naked.
Los árboles se ven desnudos en invierno. | The trees look bare in winter.
Las paredes están desnudas, necesito decorarlas. | The walls are bare, I need to decorate them.
Las montañas se ven desnudas sin vegetación. | The mountains look bare without vegetation.

191 – máximo | **maximum, greatest**

Ese es el precio máximo que puedo pagar. | That's the maximum price I can pay.
Debes dar tu máximo esfuerzo en el partido. | You should give your maximum effort in the game.
El calor llegó a su punto máximo al mediodía. | The heat reached its maximum point at noon.
La velocidad máxima en esta calle es de cuarenta. | The maximum speed on this street is 40.
Esta es mi máxima prioridad ahora mismo. | This is my top priority right now.
Tengo la máxima confianza en ti. | I have the utmost confidence in you.
Los máximos goleadores de la liga son argentinos. | The top scorers of the league are Argentinians.
Estos son los niveles máximos permitidos. | These are the maximum levels allowed.
Las medidas máximas de seguridad están activas. | Maximum security measures are in place.
Las velocidades máximas varían por zona. | Maximum speeds vary by area.

192 – decidido | **determined, decided**

El entrenador está decidido a ganar. | The coach is determined to win.
Mi hermano está decidido a estudiar medicina. | My brother is determined to study medicine.
Carlos es muy decidido con sus metas. | Carlos is very determined with his goals.
La doctora estaba decidida a ayudar. | The doctor was determined to help.
Mi hermana ya está decidida sobre el vestido. | My sister is already decided about the dress.
Mi hermana está decidida a comenzar su propio negocio. | My sister is determined to start her own business.
Los jugadores están decididos a ganar. | The players are determined to win.
Son chicos decididos. | They're determined guys.
Estamos decididas a abrir un restaurante. | We are determined to open a restaurant.
Ellas no se quedan esperando, son decididas. | They don't wait around, they are determined.

193 – grueso | **thick**

Mi abuelo tiene el cabello grueso y canoso. | My grandfather has thick, gray hair.
Necesito un colchón más grueso. | I need a thicker mattress.
El libro grueso de matemáticas pesa una tonelada. | The thick math book weighs a ton.
La pared gruesa no deja pasar el ruido. | The thick wall doesn't let noise through.
Uso una manta gruesa en invierno. | I use a thick blanket in winter.
La cuerda gruesa aguanta más peso. | The thick cord holds more weight.
Los troncos gruesos arden más lento. | Thick logs burn more slowly.
Compré unos marcadores gruesos para el póster. | I bought some thick markers for the poster.
Mis piernas se ven gruesas con estos pantalones. | My legs look thick in these pants.
Las sogas gruesas se usan en barcos. | Thick ropes are used on ships.

194 – plano | **flat, level, smooth**

El lago se ve plano como un espejo. | The lake looks flat like a mirror.
Un estómago plano es mi meta para el verano. | A flat stomach is my goal for summer.
Este terreno plano es ideal para construir. | This flat land is ideal for building.
Necesito una superficie plana para cortar la tela. | I need a flat surface to cut the fabric.
Hay gente que cree que la Tierra es plana. | There are people who believe that the Earth is flat.
Compré una televisión de pantalla plana. | I bought a flat-screen TV.
Estos zapatos planos son más cómodos. | These flat shoes are more comfortable.
Los caminos planos son ideales para correr. | Flat paths are ideal for running.
Las piedras planas son perfectas para brincar en el agua. | Flat stones are perfect for skipping across the water.
Las pantallas planas son muy comunes ahora. | Flat screens are very common now.

195 – dormido | **asleep**

Mi papá está dormido en el sofá. | My dad is asleep on the couch.
Mi hermano todavía está dormido. | My brother is still asleep.
El gato está dormido al sol en el patio. | The cat is asleep in the sun on the patio.
Me levanté con la mano dormida. | I woke up with my hand asleep.
Tu mamá ya está dormida, no la despiertes. | Your mom is already asleep, don't wake her up.
Me senté mal y ahora tengo la pierna dormida. | I sat wrong and now my leg is asleep.
Mis hijos ya están dormidos. | My kids are already asleep.
Los gatitos están dormidos junto al calentador. | The kittens are asleep next to the water heater.
Las gemelas están dormidas en la misma cama. | The twins are asleep in the same bed.
Las niñas están dormidas en el cuarto de al lado. | The girls are asleep in the next room.

196 – decente

decent

Solo quiero un médico decente que me escuche. — I just want a decent doctor who will listen to me.
Este restaurante tiene comida decente. — This restaurant has decent food.
Ponte algo decente para ir a la iglesia. — Put on something decent to go to church.
La película estuvo decente. — The movie was decent.
Busco una casa decente. — I'm looking for a decent house.
Es una propuesta decente. — It's a decent proposal.
Mis padres son personas decentes. — My parents are decent people.
Tienen modales decentes para su edad. — They have decent manners for their age.
No tenían opciones decentes para vegetarianos. — They didn't have decent options for vegetarians.
Estas son ofertas decentes. — These are decent offers.

197 – sorprendente

surprising

El resultado fue sorprendente para todos. — The result was surprising for everyone.
Hicimos un descubrimiento sorprendente. — We made a surprising discovery.
El mago hizo un truco sorprendente. — The magician did a surprising trick.
Es sorprendente que ella no haya llegado todavía. — It's surprising that she hasn't arrived yet.
Una idea sorprendente salió de nuestra charla. — A surprising idea came out of our chat.
La reacción de la niña fue sorprendente. — The girl's reaction was surprising.
Los resultados sorprendentes animaron al grupo. — The surprising results encouraged the group.
Fueron logros sorprendentes en poco tiempo. — They were surprising achievements in little time.
Escuchamos noticias sorprendentes ayer. — We heard surprising news yesterday.
Hay similitudes sorprendentes entre estos casos. — There are surprising similarities between these cases.

198 – solitario

solitary, lonely

Después del divorcio se volvió más solitario. — After the divorce he became more solitary.
Me siento solitario en esta gran ciudad. — I feel lonely in this big city.
Es un chico solitario y no le gusta socializar. — He is a lonely boy and doesn't like to socialize.
Ella es una persona solitaria. — She is a solitary person.
En la fiesta se sintió solitaria. — At the party she felt lonely.
Es una persona solitaria que disfruta caminar sola. — She's a solitary person who enjoys walking alone.
Los gatos son animales solitarios por naturaleza. — Cats are solitary animals by nature.
Los lobos solitarios cazan sin manada. — Solitary wolves hunt without a pack.
Son personas solitarias que prefieren no socializar. — They are solitary people who prefer not to socialize.
Encontramos flores solitarias en el desierto. — We found solitary flowers in the desert.

199 – crudo — **raw, harsh**

No me gusta el pescado crudo. — I don't like raw fish.
El ajo crudo es muy fuerte. — Raw garlic is very strong.
El petróleo crudo subió de precio otra vez. — Crude oil went up in price again.
No me gusta la cebolla cruda. — I don't like raw onion.
Me gusta más la zanahoria cruda que cocida. — I like raw carrots more than cooked.
Esta carne está cruda, hay que cocinarla más. — This meat is raw, it needs to be cooked more.
Los días más crudos del invierno ya pasaron. — The harshest days of winter have already passed.
No es seguro comer huevos crudos. — It's not safe to eat raw eggs.
Las almendras crudas son más nutritivas. — Raw almonds are more nutritious.
Me ofrecieron verduras crudas con salsa. — They offered me raw vegetables with dip.

200 – estupendo — **wonderful, great, stupendous**

El viaje estuvo estupendo. — The trip was wonderful.
Fue un día estupendo para ir a la playa. — It was a great day to go to the beach.
Estupendo, entonces quedamos así. — Great, so we'll leave it like that.
La película estuvo estupenda, me encantó. — The movie was wonderful, I loved it.
La vista desde aquí es estupenda. — The view from here is wonderful.
La actuación estuvo estupenda. — The performance was stupendous.
Tenemos vecinos estupendos. — We have wonderful neighbors.
Tuvimos unos guías estupendos en el tour. — We had some great guides on the tour.
Estupendas noticias del hospital. — Wonderful news from the hospital.
Las vacaciones fueron estupendas. — The vacation was wonderful.

www.ingramcontent.com/pod-product-compliance
Lightning Source LLC
LaVergne TN
LVHW080313110826
845155LV00023B/125

* 9 7 8 1 9 5 2 1 6 1 1 4 8 *